Gurcharan Das is one of India's most celebrated authors and thinkers. Among his best-selling and iconic books are *India Unbound: From Independence to the Global Information Age*; *The Difficulty of Being Good: On the Subtle Art of Dharma*; *Kama: The Riddle of Desire* and *A Sort of Freedom*. He is also general editor of a fifteen-volume series, The Story of Indian Business. His columns on current issues and philosophy are among the most widely read in the country.

The DILEMMA *of an* INDIAN LIBERAL

GURCHARAN DAS

SPEAKING TIGER BOOKS LLP
125A, Ground Floor, Shahpur Jat, near Asiad Village,
New Delhi 110049

First published by Speaking Tiger Books in 2024

ISBN: 978-93-5447-679-2
eISBN: 978-93-5447-678-5

10 9 8 7 6 5 4 3 2 1

Contents

Introduction

I became a liberal because I believed in the virtues of openness, mutual respect, and a concern for others. Liberalism offered me an ethically responsible order of human progress without necessarily involving the state. It is quite remarkable how liberalism—an idea born in 18th-century Europe—went on to become the reigning ideology of the world. For over two centuries, liberal democracies and free markets spread around the world to become the only sensible way to organise public life.

Liberalism arrived in India on the coat-tails of the British Raj but quickly found a comfortable home among educated Indians because their temper was basically liberal. From ancient times, there has existed a questioning, sceptical attitude on the subcontinent, and a quiet toleration for all beliefs in a diverse land of 330 million gods, where no god could afford to feel jealous. Typically, Indians added their own spin to it—the notion of inner freedom—thus making the European idea in their own image. The colonial masters, meanwhile, appeared oblivious to the irony of teaching liberalism to their subjects while behaving illiberally themselves.

I feel fortunate to have lived my life in a relatively peaceful liberal age under an international liberal order. But sadly, the curtain seems to be closing on this age. In the third decade of the 21st century, liberal democracy is in retreat around the world. Societies are hopelessly polarised. Many governments are being slowly captured by demagogues. Populists are on the march. Liberalism is on the decline almost everywhere, including in India. Books are appearing with titles like *Why Liberalism Failed*. Some are asking, 'Is liberalism dead?' The right believes that the fall of liberalism is due to its commitment to a 'spiritually empty freedom'. It claims that too much individualism has eroded the community and traditional values that held society together. The left blames it on global capitalism and the growth of inequality. Both blame the 'great chasm' between liberal elites and ordinary people. And I ask insistently: How could anyone give up such a sensible ideology that has liberated millions around the world from oppression and poverty?

At a time when India is rising economically and is poised to become a major global player as a democratic counterweight to dictatorial China, it is ironic that its own democratic institutions are weakening. The recent rise of identity politics, majoritarianism and Hindu nationalism presents a challenge to the Indian liberal. Critics are being silenced, the discourse in social media has become a weapon of the right wing. How to deal with a conflict between the liberal value of free speech and maintaining harmony in society? How to navigate in this polarised environment? How does a liberal deal with rising illiberalism?

There is another irony. India was once admired and envied as a vigorous democracy, but it was saddled with a poorly performing economy. The latter was the consequence of a wrong model, a socialist command economy called the 'Licence Raj'. Indians finally won their economic freedom after four decades in 1991 and India went on to become the world's second-fastest-growing economy for the next three decades. It had achieved the liberal dream—a true democracy and a free, dynamic economy. But just when everything seemed to be going well, democracy began to weaken. And the old debate has returned: political versus economic freedom.

In order to elucidate the dilemma of an Indian liberal,

I shall recount my own journey in this book—how I became a liberal. Why *my* story? Because I believe that one person's journey through life, honestly narrated, is the true data of history. During my journey I encountered many knotty dilemmas, and several of these are still unresolved. Wrestling with them has gone into the making of an Indian liberal—thus, the title of this book. While telling my story, I realise I have also narrated the story of a nation struggling to become a successful liberal democracy.

'Liberal' is a frustrating word, and I begin by defining who is a liberal in the first chapter. In Chapter 2, I recount how a modern idea, born among European philosophers in the 18th century, spread across the globe to become the world's leading ideology. In the third chapter, I trace my own liberalism back to the searching, plural, and tolerant temper in ancient India. Chapter 4 shows how this modern idea arrived in India with the British in the 19th century, and how Indian liberals quickly mushroomed in towns across the country, adding their own spin to it to make it their own idea.

Chapter 5 is the heart of the book. To those familiar with liberalism and its history, I would suggest skipping the first four chapters and jumping straight to this one. It tells the story of how I became a classical liberal. In this story of the making of an Indian liberal, I pause at 28 milestones—these are moments of liberal awakenings, lessons, and predicaments. One of these is a tale of conversion at Milestone 11, which recounts how a victim of Nehru's License Raj changes from a socialist to a liberal and joins the Swatantra Party. My favourite tale, however, is at Milestone 26. I commend it as an ethically attractive way to live in the world. There is also a parallel story running in this chapter. My personal odyssey can be read as a nation's struggle to become a liberal democracy.

In Chapter 6, I point out the shortcomings of liberalism—features with which I am uncomfortable despite my overall enthusiasm for the creed. Some of the problems of liberalism are thus of its own making, and responsible for its current troubles.

The final chapter is the culmination of this book. In it, I elaborate the dilemmas, ironies, and unresolvable difficulties faced by liberalism today. I have realised that the Indian liberal is neither electable, nor is there hope for a true liberal party. Worse, I have no one to vote for. The sad truth is that the liberal is on a lonely road.

Even though the liberal age is coming to an end, I conclude this book on a cautiously optimistic note. Amidst all the pessimism, I believe there are good reasons for hope.

Liberalism is too sensible, and it has abundant strengths, to stay down for too long. After all, it has faced and defeated far worse enemies—fascism and communism—and brought so much good to the world in the past two centuries. Its strong suit is its open-mindedness; add to it, in India's case, a liberal civilizational temper. It is easy to believe that the right sort of leaders could harness these strengths to restore the liberal creed.

Finally, this book is a personal testament, not an academic work. Since it is meant for the thoughtful lay reader, I have dispensed with irritating footnotes. I have, however, cited authors occasionally, and provided a select bibliography for readers who wish to go further into the subject.

1

Who Is a Liberal, Anyway?

In which I try and define a slippery word and the ideology that accompanies it.

Who is a liberal, anyway? The word comes from the Latin *liber*, which means 'free'. Liberals believe in liberty. But so does everyone else. So, that's not very helpful. At a personal level, a liberal is an open-minded, generous, and tolerant person, who is open to new ideas. When presented with evidence to the contrary, the liberal is apt to change his mind. A liberal's temper tends to be suspicious of political, military and theocratic power. When confronted with someone of the opposite belief, the liberal has the ability to show respect and even value the opponent's creed. (The true story at the end of Chapter 5—at Milestone 26: 'How to Live in the World'—is an example of this.)

A liberal political order provides the rule of law and maximum equal liberty to its citizens. It protects individual rights and civil liberties, and places limits on state power. It is based on consent, achieved through the institutions of liberal democracy. A liberal economic order depends on market outcomes, on private property rather than state ownership, but accepts the value of market regulation. There is a difference between political and economic liberalism. A person can be politically liberal without being economically liberal.

Liberalism has been the dominant ideology of the modern age, although political liberalism has been more widely adopted than economic liberalism. The liberal landscape, however, is confusing and slippery. There are classical liberals, modern liberals, left liberals, neoliberals, libertarians, and more. Around 1900, the word 'liberal' underwent a change as a result of a series of depressions and mass unemployment in America. A group called the 'progressives', who advocated state intervention to fix this problem, started calling themselves 'modern liberals'. There was irony here—the critics of economic freedom and limited government had appropriated the label. Today, they are known as left liberals or social democrats. They are generally politically liberal but not economically liberal.

Libertarians are more ideological than classical liberals. They are absolutist about freedom, preferring a minimal or a 'night-watchman state'. Classical liberals are more pragmatic and moderate in comparison. Not only do they want the state to provide law and order, they also support state spending for public goods, especially education and health, although they don't think the state needs necessarily to *run* schools and hospitals. Many also accept a safety net for the poorest. I am a classical liberal.

'Neoliberal' entered the vocabulary as a reaction to the problems created by the welfare state after the 1970s. Margaret Thatcher in the UK and Ronald Reagan in America were its standard bearers, who helped reform the relationship between the market and the state, and sold 'economic freedom' tirelessly to the public in the 1980s. The left believes that neoliberals care more about liberty than equality and have an excessive faith in the market. At the other end of the political spectrum, right-wing nationalists disapprove of the neoliberal's attachment to free trade and globalisation, which has weakened local bonds and traditions.

Liberalism's ideas are also in opposition to conservatism. Conservatives look to the past; liberals to the future. Conservatives believe in stability, tradition, and the existing social order, including its hierarchies. Unlike liberals, they find value in the ways—or supposed ways—of their ancestors and are suspicious of many ideas of modernity; they put their faith in the old virtues of duty, deference and obedience.

The chief rival of liberalism is socialism. Socialists generally value equality over liberty and include all sorts of collectivists—Utopians, Marxists, labour unionists and social democrats. The starting point of Marxists is class conflict, which they believe can only be resolved by ending economic inequality. Socialists divide themselves between the patient and impatient. The impatient want a radical transformation of society in a revolutionary leap, while the patient prefer gradual reform through democratic institutions. Both hope for a postcapitalist society of common ownership and material equality. In their eyes, liberalism's respect for private property stands in the way of true progress.

Liberalism's enemy is fascism, a far-right political ideology that believes in a strong, 'muscular' state. Fascism is authoritarian and looks to a dictator to bring about militaristic order and obedience in society. It is also generally ultra-nationalist. It does not accept dissent, and forcibly suppresses all opposition. It subordinates the individual's interest for what it believes is the greater good of the nation or race. A liberal, on the other hand, is suspicious of all nationalisms, whether religious, linguistic or ethnic.

2

A Short History of a Modern Idea

In which I narrate briefly the history of the modern idea of liberalism, from the 18th-century European Enlightenment to the present, and how it became the reigning ideology of the world.

Classical liberalism

Liberalism began as a philosophical idea during Europe's Age of Enlightenment in the 18th century, embracing the values of reason and science, human dignity, free thinking and protection of an individual's freedom. From these values, it went on to become a political movement which sought to replace the restraints imposed on human freedom by the establishment—that is, by the landed aristocracy, the state religion and absolute monarchy. The Glorious Revolution in England (1688), the American Revolution (1776) and the French Revolution (1789), all employed these liberal ideas to overthrow their respective establishments in varying degrees. From there, liberalism went on to become the reigning ideology of the world, and it has largely shaped the political history of the past two and half centuries.

Liberals believe that the state is necessary to protect individuals from harm, including harm from the state. John Locke, the English philosopher and father of modern liberalism, asserted in 1690 in his *Two Treatises* that the individual has the right to resist unjust authority. What made a government legitimate, he said, was *consent* of the people. This could be achieved through consensus; and this led to the idea of voting, majority rule and a liberal democracy. Early liberals believed, however, that not everyone was competent to vote, and they restricted the franchise. Over time, the franchise expanded gradually to become universal, as it is today.

With their commitment to freedom, liberals wanted to ensure that people had the ability to live their lives freely and privately in peace. Thus was born the idea of fundamental rights of all citizens—such as the right to life, free thought, speech, association and freedom from arbitrary arrest—and these rights were later guaranteed in modern constitutions. Liberals were also concerned with the danger of unchecked force of the majority. Hence came the separation of powers of the state—the legislature, the executive and the judiciary—and a legislature divided between an upper and a lower house. This system of checks and balances was first embodied in the American Constitution, written in 1787.

The economic foundations of liberalism too were laid in Britain, where a major source of oppression was the feudal nature of land ownership. John Locke developed a theory of property to protect individuals from coercion. He argued that a person transforms land through his labour, and in this manner the land becomes his own. Individuals thus acquire a right to property by their labour. By means of this right, they sustain the most important of all rights—the right to life. Through this logic, the right to property became a central doctrine of liberalism.

In the 18th century, monarchs in Europe were forever fighting for supremacy based on the misguided notion in international trade that gain for one country means a loss for another. Based on this mercantilist theory, governments intervened constantly, fixing tariffs and meddling with prices to protect their industries from foreign competition. In Britain, however, monarchs were frustrated in parliament by liberals in the Whig party, who challenged these false mercantilist assumptions. Based on the ideas of the Scottish economist and philosopher Adam Smith, detailed in *The Wealth of Nations* (1776), liberals argued that free trade benefits all parties—that competition is good, for it leads to the production of more and better goods, resulting in lowering of prices; and when individuals pursue their self-interest through trade, it brings about a division of labour that enhances the welfare of the whole through what Smith termed an 'invisible hand'.

Liberalism spreads around the world

These liberal ideas caught the world's imagination in country after country, and they spread and became part of modernity. In the late 18th and 19th centuries, liberal governments came up in Europe and the Americas. Based on these ideas, France abolished feudalism and monarchy. America won its independence from the British Crown; years later, it also ended slavery after a bloody civil war. Liberal agitations in Latin America brought independence from imperial Spain and Portugal. In the Middle East, liberal reform in the Ottoman Empire created a crisis in

Islam that continues to this day. The liberal momentum continued in the 20th century when Russia overthrew the Tsar, the bastion of autocracy. The Allied victory in the First World War ended four empires in Europe, marking a liberal triumph across the European continent. The Second World War defeated the illiberal ideology of fascism.

Soon after the Second World War, India won its independence without shedding an ounce of blood, thanks to a liberal freedom movement led by M.K. Gandhi. Other colonised countries in Asia and Africa followed suit in a deluge of decolonisation. They all adopted liberal democratic constitutions, hoping this would usher in the same freedoms and prosperity as of the West. The results, however, were mixed, with democracy taking root in some countries but not in others; and some countries developed faster economically than others. When the Soviet Union collapsed in 1991, the victory of liberalism was complete, having defeated its last major enemy after fascism—namely, communism.

Liberalism created two international economic orders, each culminating in the globalisation of capitalism. The first liberal order was promoted by the British in the late 19th century in the wake of technological transformations of the Industrial Revolution, as transport and communication costs dropped dramatically through the railways, steamship and the telegraph. It brought about free mobility of commodities, capital and labour. Britain sponsored the legal framework of free trade, international property rights, the gold standard and a payments system based in London. Other states reciprocated by lowering tariffs, and globalisation became a reality as national economies were joined through international trade in goods.

The United States helped create a second liberal international order after the allied victory in the Second World War, founding the United Nations and the Bretton Woods institutions—GATT (followed by WTO), IMF and the World Bank. The US also resurrected the economic ideas of the first liberal order, advocating free trade, the gold standard and free capital mobility. It championed human rights in large measure, and succeeded in bringing relative peace and prosperity to the free world. With the fall of the Iron Curtain across Eastern Europe in 1989 and, finally, the collapse of the Soviet Union, many more nations around the world embraced the liberal order based on free markets and democratic self-government.

Modern liberalism

The Industrial Revolution produced great wealth and a middle class in the 19th century, but it also brought discontent. Capitalism concentrated wealth in the hands of a few and the masses failed to benefit commensurately. The discontent also had to do with the market economy's tendency to work in boom-and-bust cycles. The worst bust came in the 1930s when a worldwide depression threatened the very survival of democratic capitalism. The US President Franklin D. Roosevelt (FDR) responded with a New Deal (1933-39) which provided emergency assistance, temporary jobs, placed restrictions on banking, gave more power to trade unions and established a social security programme. The British economist John Maynard Keynes, in his influential *The General Theory of Employment, Interest and Money* (1936), lent intellectual respectability to this massive government intervention. Thus, a new offshoot of liberalism known as progressivism came into being.

At the end of the Second World War, there was an unusual coming together of democracy and liberalism. After surviving the collapse from the Great Depression of the 1930s, then defeating fascism in the World War, liberal democracy went on to experience a heyday in the second half of the 20th century. For the decolonised, newly-independent countries liberated in the War—many of which had witnessed the horrors of totalitarianism and fascism—liberal democracy became the logical choice.

Inspired by FDR and Keynes, liberal democracies re-invented themselves, creating the modern welfare state. They expanded programmes to provide not only the usual forms of social insurance but also pensions, unemployment benefits, subsidised medical care, family allowances and state-funded university education. Scandinavian countries went further, to provide 'cradle to grave' security. Thus, the word 'liberal' took on the additional meaning of someone who supported government intervention for social welfare. This new form of liberalism is sometimes called progressivism, or modern liberalism or left liberalism. By the 1990s, the conservative right in American politics was using 'liberal' as a term of abuse for almost anyone who disagreed with it.

Neoliberalism

After decades of prosperity following the Second World War, economic growth slowed down around the world, especially in the West, in the mid-1970s due to a number of reasons, ranging from the 1973 oil crisis and the Vietnam War to the fall of the Bretton Woods system and rising inflation in the US. This presented a challenge to liberalism. It became difficult to support the welfare state. The cost of maintaining it pushed governments to untenable levels of taxation and debt. This in turn brought about a revival of classical liberalism under the name of neoliberalism. This time around, people looked to the Austrian-born British economist F.A. Hayek and the American economist Milton Friedman as their intellectual gurus. Although they differed in some ways, fundamentally, Hayek and Friedman believed in the superiority of the free market, and that welfare planning would never work.

In politics, Prime Minister Margaret Thatcher in Britain and President Ronald Reagan in the United States led the ideological charge during the 1980s. At the same time, in the East, Deng Xiaoping began liberalising communist China from a closed backwater to a dynamic capitalist economy. The fall of the Berlin Wall in 1989 and the collapse of the Soviet Union in 1991 contributed to the neoliberal momentum. In the summer of that year, far-reaching liberal reforms also occurred in India.

Then followed almost two decades of unprecedented globalisation under the so-called 'Washington Consensus'. This tilted the global balance in favour of the market, which reigned supreme for a generation under the neoliberal belief that human well-being was best advanced by liberating entrepreneurial energies under an institutional framework characterised by property rights, free markets and free trade.

The present crisis of liberalism

The neoliberal euphoria did not last and today, in the third decade of the 21st century, liberalism is under siege. Thirty years ago, it had appeared that liberalism had won its final victory. At the fall of the Iron Curtain, both its major rival ideologies had been defeated—fascism in the Second World War and communism in 1989—and it seemed as though human civilisation had reached the end of its socio-political evolution. Some even called it the 'end of history'. Yet today, anti-liberalism has become pervasive. From the middle of the second decade of the 21st century, democracy has been in retreat worldwide. Thuggish populists believe that freedom is overrated, and majorities are being led by ambitious demagogues. Authoritarianism is on the march. The Indian liberal is concerned with the rise of Hindu nationalism and the weakening of democracy. The global Left believes that liberalism is exhausted, unable to cope with inequalities, corporate power and environmental degradation. The right blames liberalism for the collapse of traditional values, rampant criminality and disrespect for authority, which is seen as essential for political stability and order, and which in turn is regarded as a prerequisite for economic progress.

How did this come to pass? There is no easy answer. One view is that liberals got distracted by the paranoia of the Cold War in the second half of the 20th century. Instead of evolving their emancipatory creed, they became obsessed with the enemy—communism. This was 'liberalism of fear' as the Harvard professor Judith Shklar called it in the 1960s. It prompted America to back authoritarian regimes in Latin America and take the fight into the 'killing fields' of Asia. It prevented Cold War liberals from seizing the opportunity in 1989 to rethink the core commitments and the promise of their creed, instead of merely celebrating their geopolitical triumph.

The first shock after the triumph came on 11 September 2001 with the terrorist bombing of the twin towers in New York when a competing Islamic ideology challenged the liberal political order, and made it insecure. A second shock came with a global financial crisis in 2008, which shook people's faith in the economic system of the liberal order, and inequality of the market system became the target. The discontent came to a head in the middle of the second decade with the rise of populism and nationalism in different parts of the world. In the United States and

Britain, rising anti-liberal sentiment both on the right and the left began to shatter some of the exalted ideals of liberal democracy and free markets. The sentiment began to win popular political support around 2015, leading to Brexit in Britain and Donald Trump's presidency in America. In India, the pervasive corruption in the UPA government, which had been in power since 2004, led to the rise of a right-wing Hindu nationalist government. These challenges spread quickly around the world, affecting countries as dissimilar as Hungary, Poland, Turkey and Brazil.

With the demise of communism, there is no longer a viable alternative to the market to organise economic life. Hence, capitalism's critics have turned to reforming it, to 'humanising' it. One of the most persuasive efforts is that of the Nobel Prize-winning economist-philosopher Amartya Sen, whose argument in this regard is best understood from his book *Development as Freedom*. It entails extending the meaning of the word 'freedom'. In ordinary English, freedom means to be free of obstacles in the path of an individual, or having the ability to choose between alternatives. A second meaning proposed by Sen is to be 'free to do something or become capable of doing it'. Freedom from want or poverty enhances one's capability to act. So do good education, good nutrition and good health;

they allow an individual to live a better life. The older meaning of 'freedom' is renamed 'negative freedom', and the new is called 'positive freedom'. The distinction is not merely academic. It is a cry for action—an imperative for the state to provide good education, nutrition and health to all citizens.

Although this thesis enhances the power of the state, the classical liberal in me finds it persuasive. I find it difficult to counter this redefinition of liberty because it, in fact, enhances the core liberal values of freedom of the individual and justice in society.

Conclusion

Liberalism may be under siege today, but it has stood the test of time. It has been the reigning ideology in much of the world ever since modernity began more than two hundred years ago. This is not surprising because it has helped to unshackle humanity of feudal hierarchies based on status and tradition. It has brought unprecedented economic opportunities, affording social mobility to the ordinary person. It has embedded liberal democracy in the world as the preferred political order, giving voice to millions.

The competing claims of the state and the market have been a common refrain in liberalism's story. Both the state and the market evolved in parallel during the 19th century when the Industrial Revolution brought a new order. There were times when the state and the market collaborated; at other times, they behaved like rivals. Before 1930, markets grew unchecked under a laissez-faire belief. Then they capsized during the Great Depression, when the state had to become saviour and a new liberalism was born. In the second half of the 20th century the free market and the welfare state both grew and it seemed as though the right balance had been found. When growth stopped in the 1970s, the balance tilted back to the market under the neoliberal flag. Now, once again, the balance is tilting towards the state. The lesson is that both market power and state power need to check each other. Sometimes, the state disciplines the market; at other times, the market tames the state. Emasculating the market is not liberal; nor is vice versa. It is an uneasy balance.

Liberalism has stood for different things at different times. Like any ideology, it has had its share of critics. In the eyes of the left, the classical liberal is an uncaring slave of the market. The right abuses the left liberal, referring to him as a socialist in disguise. Despite the confusion and animosity, the core convictions of liberalism—liberty, equality, self-dependence—have made sense to people around the world and given them hope for a better future.

3

The Indian Temper Is Liberal

In which I discover that Indians have always been infuriatingly liberal—what else do you expect in a land of 330 million gods where none can afford to be jealous!

Many think that 'liberal' is a Western idea when in fact it is a universal sentiment shared by all human beings. Liberalism is not just a set of beliefs or policies, it is a temperament. It is a disposition open to complexity, willing to acknowledge uncertainty, tolerant of differences, and resistant to bullying.

The Indian temper, I find, has always been plural, tolerant, democratic and liberal. It originates in the earliest sacred text of the subcontinent, the *Rig Veda* (c.1500 BCE). In the charming humility of its Nasadiya verse (10.129), it raises the question: how was the cosmos created?

> *[In the beginning] there was neither being nor non-being...[but] who really knows?...[for] the gods came afterwards.*

After some back and forth, it concludes that perhaps no one, not even the creator, knows how the cosmos came into being. Here, then, is the birth of Vedic scepticism. This questioning attitude may have led to the invention of the creator god in the *Rig Veda* whose name was the interrogative Sanskrit pronoun 'Ka', or 'Who?'

This searching attitude is also reflected in the '*Neti, neti*' ('Not this, not that') method of enquiry in the mental experiments of the Upanishads. By negating, one by one, everything that is not real, a person eventually negates all objects of consciousness, including thoughts and the mind, and is left only with what is real. Thus, one understands the nature of reality. When a new student comes to a teacher (as Sarvepalli Radhakrishnan reminds us in *The Hindu Way of Life*), the teacher asks him about his favourite god, or *ishtadevata*. It is a natural question because the peoples of the Indian subcontinent belonged to different communities, worshipped different gods and practised different rituals. The Vedanta teacher then tells the student that our many gods are merely symbols of the one Absolute within us.

India truly is a 'museum of beliefs and a medley of rites' that have coexisted democratically over many centuries. It has an amazing ability to absorb the customs and ideas of its diverse peoples, transforming them into something new. Many aboriginal gods entered the fold—like Kali, a non-Aryan god who went on to become the 'compassionate mother of the universe' and was identified with the supreme Godhead. Some tribes had mystic animals, who became vehicles and companions of the gods. Thus, Shiva mounts a bull, Surya a horse, Saraswati a swan, Lakshmi an owl, Kartikeya a peacock, Ganesha a mouse, and so on. Hanuman, the monkey-general of Ram, reflects the synthesis of early nature gods with later devotional theism. In the epics, the non-Aryan Krishna triumphs over Indra, the king of Vedic gods. The non-Vedic Shiva, similarly, triumphs over the Vedic Daksha, when the latter's own daughter, Sati, falls in love with Shiva. The image of Harihara, one half Vishnu and one half Shiva, satisfies both Vaishnavites, who believe in the supremacy of Vishnu, and Shaivites, who believe that Shiva is the Supreme God.

In a land of 330 million gods, no god can afford to feel jealous. Thus, the gods bequeathed to humans their own liberal temper.

A diverse people learned to live together partially because none had a dominating god, nor an overbearing prophet. The oldest major faiths, Hinduism and Buddhism, had no single authoritative book. Since a hierarchical church was also absent, there was no notion of heresy. This is why the Indian idea of secularism is not separation of church and state but a respect for all religions. To despise other people's gods is to despise oneself, says one of Ashoka's inscriptions. Each person, every group or tribe has an individuality that is worthy of reverence, and deserves to live in a state of maximum freedom. This epitomises the secular liberal Indian temper, which is especially needed at this time in the country's history. At its root lies the Indian ability to make a seemingly bizarre claim in a single breath: there are many gods, and only one God. It is, in fact, the Upanishadic teacher's message to the student: the many gods are merely different names for the Absolute. Thus, polytheism is transformed into monism. In the same way, India's maddening diversity of blood, colour, language, dress, manners and sects becomes a profound civilisational unity. What matters in the end is conduct, not belief.

The liberal temper is reflected in the philosophical scepticism of famous philosophers of competing doctrines—Dignaga, Shabara, Kumarila, Dharmakirti. It centred around the epistemological question of *pramana*: how do we know what we know? Each one concludes that the only sure source of knowledge is perception and inference. Thus, they cannot trust either faith or scripture, whether Vedic or Buddhist, and are particularly critical of superstition and the supernatural. Heaven, in short, does not exist. These claims were significant because these philosophers belonged to the prestigious schools of Nyaya, Sankhya, and even the conservative Mimamsa. This liberal questioning seems to have occurred in a remarkable 'age of reason' between the 5th and 7th centuries CE. The Sanskritist Lawrence McCrea of Cornell University calls it an 'Early Indian Enlightenment'.

Another way to appreciate India's temper is to compare it with China's. China's history is a story of empires. India's is of competing kingdoms. India had four empires—Maurya, Gupta, Mughal and British—but they were weaker than the weakest Chinese empire. China had a strong state and a weak society. India's was the opposite—a weak state and a strong society. The emperor gave and interpreted the law in China. In India, the law, or dharma, preceded the king, and the king's duty, *rajdharma*, was to uphold the law for the benefit of the people. And the interpreter of the law was the brahmin. Thus, early on, India had a liberal division of powers that weakened the state. The emperor owned the land in China. The *Arthashastra* is at pains to remind the king in India that he does not own the land but has a right to one sixth of the produce, *shat bhaga*, and that too is contingent on his providing public goods—law and order, an army, roads and other infrastructure. Given a weak state, oppression in India did not come from the state but from society, for example, from high-caste brahmins. The liberators from oppression were heterodox sects like the Buddhists and egalitarian gurus who taught the message of bhakti.

India possessed a liberal, optimistic attitude towards sexual desire as well. It begins early, in the ancient *Rig Veda*, where the cosmos is created from the seed of kama, 'desire'. The Veda thinks of kama as a life force, an animating principle. Ancient Indians elevated desire to a *purushartha*, 'an aim of life', and even believed in a deity named Kama, the god of desire. The great god Krishna was a favourite lover. On hearing his flute, women of Vrindavan sneaked out of their homes into the forest and danced the raas-leela with their lover-god through an entire Brahma night lasting 4.5 billion years. Krishna multiplied himself so that each woman believed she was dancing exclusively with him.

This optimistic spirit reached a peak in the courts of the Gupta Empire, between 320 CE and 550 CE, when a sexual liberation seems to have occurred. The life force, kama, became a romantic orientation to the world, spreading through the psychological life of human beings. This period has bequeathed an impressive legacy of erotic culture—of the *Kamasutra,* love poetry and sculpture.

But there is also a pessimistic strand of desire in Indian tradition. Some of the Dharma texts are restrictive in dealing with sex and desire. The *sanyasi*, or renouncer, looms large in the Indian imagination, offering the householder an alternative lifestyle. To him, sexuality is an ever-present threat. The epics and puranas are full of temptations of heavenly *apsaras*, or nymphs. The renouncer fears an involuntary ejaculation of semen, a precious life-force from which life is created and which is akin to spiritual energy.

The divide between kama optimists and pessimists reflects the dual nature of human beings—the erotic and the ascetic in all of us. It is yet another example of the nuance and pluralism that inform Indian thought and tradition.

But I must moderate this mostly positive account of the Indian spirit by noting that India did not institutionalise crucial elements of liberalism such as the rule of law and equality. In fact, the social institution of caste is an illiberal side to the national character. People everywhere need to feel superior to others; hierarchy is inescapable. But only in India was inequality sanctified by religion. Status was determined at birth; it decided your occupation; it did not allow some people to sit and eat together, nor tolerate marriages between them. There has been a great effort since Independence to end this inequality by a mostly liberal state. But elitism is hard to eliminate and so discrimination continues, and it remains part of the Indian temper.

Let me close with the oft repeated but always inspiring notion of *Vasudhaiva Kutumbakam*. It is a liberal idea which means that the whole world is one family. It is an apt way to end this chapter because the bad old 19th-century European-style nationalism is rearing its ugly head both in India and the world. The rise of Hindu nationalism today presents a challenge to India's secular ideal of 'respect for all religions' and its essentially liberal temper. *Vasudhaiva Kutumbakam*, today, is thus not merely an historic ideal to be cherished, but a call to action.

4

The Modern Idea Comes to India

In which the modern idea of liberalism arrives in India on the coat-tails of the Raj. Indians typically put their own spin on the idea and it evolved under the bright Indian sun.

It is one thing to have a liberal temper and quite another to adopt a modern European ideology. Liberalism arrived in India on the coat-tails of the British Raj in the early 19th century, giving Indians a fresh, new lens to look at their private and public lives, and ask how these could be improved. Liberalism here began with social reform.

The second phase was focused on political independence, when liberals demanded freedom from despotic and racist colonial rule. They succeeded in gaining independence in 1947. The transfer of power to the Indian people and framing of the Constitution to form a republic was a peak liberal moment in India's history. The Indian Constitution, with its main ideals of Justice, Liberty, Equality and Fraternity, was among the most enlightened and progressive documents in the democratic history of the world.

After Independence, Indian liberals turned their attention to economic freedom. It was a natural response to a socialist, command economy set up by Nehru's government. Thus was born the short-lived Swatantra Party in the late 1950s. It was a true liberal party but it got wiped out by the Indira Gandhi wave of the 1970s.

Indian liberalism thus has a rich and long history of social reform, political struggle and economic liberalisation. Liberals helped to re-empower fellow Indians during a period when they were politically unfree. They demanded the right to dissent against the colonial government—they wanted a free press. They tried to get Indians into government jobs, on grand juries and later into state legislatures. They insisted on education, especially of women. They strove to reform their own society from some of the most corrupt practices that had crept in.

In typical fashion, Indians were not content with just adopting a foreign ideology. They went on to improvise, put an Indian spin on it, concluding that liberal freedom was not merely 'outer' economic and political independence, but an 'inner' freedom that needed self-transformation. Indian liberalism thus became a component of a good, flourishing human life.

Liberalism evolves in India

Liberalism evolved through a number of phases. Raja Ram Mohan Roy (1772-1833) was the first significant figure to embrace this humanitarian ideal, and he inspired a whole generation of those who adopted early this modern idea. He waged a relentless campaign against the Hindu orthodoxy, especially the repugnant social institution of sati, which forced a widow to immolate herself on the funeral pyre of her husband. Like other Indian liberals, who followed him, he traced the principles of liberalism to ancient ideas in the Vedas and the Upanishads. A religious, social and educational reformer, he is sometimes known as the 'maker of modern India.'

At the next stage, in the late 19th and early 20th centuries, the attention of Indian liberals turned to political independence. Adding to the humiliation of foreign rule was horror at a spate of devastating famines in the second half of the 19th century (in which 28.8 million people died, according to one British estimate). It came on top of a sense of hopelessness caused by the collapse of India's largest industry—handloom textiles—which could no longer compete with products of Britain's industrial revolution, and brought mass impoverishment to millions of weavers. Liberals like R.C. Dutt and K.T. Telang blamed India's dire economic predicament on Britain's free trade ideology. Dadabhai Naoroji referred to free trade as a garb for the exploitative nature of British rule. He went on to win a parliamentary seat for William Gladstone's Liberal Party. As an MP in the House of Commons, he fought tirelessly to make the British public aware of the 'drain of wealth' from India and the hardships faced by his countrymen because of Britain's mercantilist policies. The Indian liberal's political response was to found the Indian National Congress (INC) in 1885 to fight for political freedom. It brought together an impressive array of liberals from all walks of life. Naoroji served as its president a number of times over the next 25 years. A liberal party was also founded in 1910, made of distinguished, moderate individuals like Tej Bahadur Sapru and V. Srinivasa Sastri. They preferred gradual change via constitutional reform, some kind of local self-government within the Empire on the model of Canada or Australia. Many of these liberals, however, began to downplay the 'liberal' label. A lot of them were beneficiaries of the favours of the Raj, others were complicit in caste privileges and religious communalism, and their gradualist approach to political freedom was regarded by many as appeasement of colonialism.

Although important, these movements for political freedom didn't go anywhere, however, until Mohandas Gandhi arrived on the scene in 1915. He led the Congress, inspiring the masses by articulating the liberal ideals of liberty and equality in the language of dharma. He also invented an amazingly non-violent methodology, *satyagraha,* which unnerved the British and went on to later inspire the civil rights movement in the United States and the movement against apartheid in South Africa.

India won its freedom in 1947 without bloodshed through a struggle that was inclusive, democratic and liberal. Not surprisingly, liberalism became the underlying ideology of free India. The Constitution provided for extensive rights and freedoms, and tried to bridge the ethnic, linguistic, caste and religious fault lines of a hugely diverse society. Middle-class Indians began to use liberal ideas to make sense of a world which was changing rapidly. But too many stepped unthinkingly into the shoes of the departing 'white sahibs' at Independence and didn't bother to reform colonial institutions or fashion a new modernity truer to the spirit of a free nation. Nor did the post-Independence elite bother to sell the Constitution to the masses, who still believe that 'it fell one day from heaven'.

Pakistan too was born at the same time from the partition of India. The Pakistan Movement was not the work of religious fanatics but of distinguished Muslim liberals, many of them educated in Britain and at Aligarh Muslim University. The crusade originated in the 19th century with Syed Ahmad Khan, who initially supported Hindu-Muslim unity but later became a champion of the two-nation theory and of Muslim nationalism. He was an accomplished Muslim intellectual and educationist, who was influenced by the ideas of the English liberal philosopher John Stuart Mill. He brought a questioning, scientific spirit to Islam and attempted to modernise and reform it. Orthodox Muslims denounced him at the time and brought over 500 fatwas against him. In the 20th century, the Pakistan Movement was also pushed by—besides the Muslim League—liberals like Muhammed Iqbal, Choudhary Rahmat Khan, and Muhammad Ali Jinnah, the founder of Pakistan.

Indians add a spin to an imported idea

When Gandhi defined freedom as 'swaraj', he explained that true liberty is 'when we learn to rule ourselves'. Inner 'self-rule' meant becoming worthy of self-government. He was not merely concerned with 'external freedom' from British rule but also with an internal freedom that made one a better human being. Denis Dalton, in a recent book, *Indian Ideas of Freedom,* argues that it was not only Gandhi but many of his great liberal contemporaries in the early 20th century who also sought an 'inner freedom'. Vivekananda, Aurobindo Ghose, Rabindranath Tagore, B.R. Ambedkar, and Jayaprakash Narayan added an ethical and spiritual dimension to the Western liberal ideal, incorporating, consciously or unconsciously, the ancient Indian ideal of inner emancipation or self-actualisation.

True to the old liberal Indian temper, liberals in India looked to their Indic traditions and innovated upon a Western ideal and gave it a dimension suited to their own character. If the genius of the West expresses itself in the relationship between the individual and the world, and if East Asia is preoccupied with the relationship between two individuals, India's intelligence finds expression in the relationship between an individual and himself or herself. So, it isn't surprising that the liberal quest for freedom in

India involved a deep inner search for *moksha*, 'liberation', within one's self that is connected with transforming society. It thus makes sense why Gandhi insisted on a pre-eminent role for ethics in public life; means to him were as important as ends. It also explains his Buddha-like obsession with *ahimsa*, or non-violence.

It is the same with the other great liberals. Ram Mohan Roy linked his liberalism with the Vedantic ideas of sharing, generosity and compassion (*mudita, udartavad* and *karuna*). Tagore thought of true nationalism as shedding an inner 'slave mentality', which had been a creation of foreign rule. Vivekananda felt the fight for self-government required one 'to raise the self by the self' as a form of spiritual freedom, and the greatest lesson in his life was 'to pay attention to the means of work, not to its end.' Aurobindo Ghose, a radical hot-head who became a mystic, was also concerned with the means of action. He believed that political freedom was based on 'moral improvement of the race'. According to Ambedkar, freedom meant liberation from the shackles of the caste system, especially upliftment of the lowest Dalit, and he too found inspiration from Buddhism.

Means and ends and non-violence are two common themes among these men. When in 1953 Jawaharlal Nehru looked back on India's freedom struggle, he concluded that its essential quality was to lay stress on means. When I think about it 75 years later, I am struck by the bravery of these men—it must have taken enormous courage to resist the world's biggest empire non-violently. What can be more liberal than their absolute conviction to fight and defeat injustice, and yet their refusal to counter immorality with immorality, hate with hate?

The original sin of liberalism

The irony of the British empire preaching liberalism while practising conquest was not lost on Indian liberals. Liberalism rose at the time when European powers were practising white supremacy, slavery, genocide and imperialism. The colonial empire in India was founded on highly illiberal acts of violent, bloody military subjugation of the subcontinent. Even in the economic sphere, the East India Company's monopoly on trade was offensive to Ram Mohan Roy's liberal sensibilities.

Liberal shibboleths about progress helped recast colonial conquests as a civilising mission. The attitude of Whites to the non-white people of the colonies was racist—'higher' races had a duty to civilise the 'lower' races. The Nobel Prize winner Rudyard Kipling celebrated the civilizing of inferior races as the 'White Man's Burden':

Take up the White Man's burden—
And reap his old reward:
The blame of those ye better,
The hate of those ye guard.

It is even more paradoxical that one of the most influential classical liberal thinkers in the 19th century, John Stuart Mill, believed that non-whites were inferior human beings and not yet ready for the benefits of liberalism or self-government. The natives needed a paternal colonial power to help reform their barbaric, superstitious society and teach them the liberal virtues of freedom, democracy and equality. He wrote a classic essay, 'On Liberty', but concluded that pre-modern cultures were not yet ready for it. Despotism, in the meanwhile, was a more suitable form of government for these 'backward' societies. It was a similar impetus that led the liberal Thomas Babington Macaulay to make an impassioned plea in 1835 to provide education in English in order to civilise Indians.

The contradiction between liberalism and empire did not faze the colonisers. Critics of liberalism have called this racist, imperial mindset the 'original sin of liberalism'. However, racism, white supremacy and imperialism are not flaws of liberalism. A non-liberal can also be racist; a non-liberal can also harbour imperial ambitions. The irony in this story is that this sin of liberalism prepared liberal Indians to turn the tables on their colonisers in the 20th century with ammunition provided by the same colonisers in terms of ideas, and they eventually won Independence by 'liberal' means. While they drew upon India's civilisational traditions to build a unique strategy for the freedom movement, Gandhi and other leaders also challenged the British Empire using the arguments of Britain's own liberal philosophers.

The one illiberal gene

The liberal architect of India's Constitution, B.R. Ambedkar, once wondered if liberal democracy was 'only a top-dressing on an Indian soil which is essentially undemocratic'. He predicted that on the day that India became a republic, 'it will be entering into a life of contradictions'. The contradiction he was thinking about originated from another original sin that occurred around the beginning of the first millennium when the mixing between the Indian people stopped suddenly. This is when the caste system became rigid according to the recent science of population genetics.

The liberal in India faces a special challenge. While there is social hierarchy everywhere in the world, in India it is sanctioned by religious belief. According to the doctrine of karma, you are born high or low based on your past deeds. Hence, Indians are more tolerant of inequality, and society is stratified more by caste than by class. After Independence, liberals like Ambedkar tried to dismantle it through laws and legislation, but social hierarchy based on caste is hard to eliminate because the beliefs that sanction it are deeply ingrained. Hence, discrimination persists despite the biggest affirmative action programme in the world.

When Ambedkar speculated about the future of the Indian Republic, he was speaking from personal experience. Born into the lowest Mahar caste, he had suffered humiliation all his life from the upper-caste elites. He had educated himself against great odds and earned prestigious degrees from the best universities in the world. He became a classical liberal and applied his intellectual and academic training to begin a heroic battle against caste inequalities, trying to provide a dignified place to the lowest 'untouchable' castes in society and politics. Just before he died in 1956, he went further: he shunned Hinduism and embraced Buddhism alongside thousands of his followers, beginning thus a new socio-religious revolution in India. Today, he is mythicised and is an iconic superhero, a 'messiah of the Dalits' who challenged the mighty Brahminical elite and liberated the depressed masses from the dark of servitude, illiteracy and powerlessness. To the country's credit, there there has been impressive social reform in the past 75 years, inspired by liberals like B.R. Ambedkar.

Rise and fall of the Swatantra Party

Free India never had unbounded faith in free trade or the liberating power of the market. The plunder of the East India Company was always a sobering reminder. A majority of Indian citizens, especially in the first decades after Independence, did not share John Stuart Mill's deep distrust of the state and of bureaucracy. It was also a socialist age worldwide when India won its freedom. Not surprisingly, the country's ethos turned in that direction. The Prime Minister, Jawaharlal Nehru, a staunch socialist, wanted to create a compassionate, egalitarian socialist society. But the Indian bureaucracy gave him a command economy that C. Rajagopalachari (Rajaji) called 'Permit-License Raj'. Meanwhile, the left wing of the Congress Party went further and demanded complete abolition of landownership.

Classical liberals became quickly disenchanted with the

government's lurch towards socialism and hence their focus turned to economic freedom. They formed the Swatantra Party under the leadership of Rajaji, which quickly became the leading opposition in the mid-sixties. Rajaji spoke thus about the command economy in 1965:

> *Controlled production, controlled prices, and other similar controls mean in the ultimate analysis controlling of persons. Under a controlled economy, it is persons, not things, who are told by some persons who are collectively called government what they must or must not do. It is this that goes contrary to respect for human personality, gradually robs the victims of the will to be free, and develops in the government a hunger for owning slaves... The State is becoming a giant entity by itself, menacingly poised against the citizen, interfering with his life at all points, mistrusting the people, imposing restrictions, introducing a series of controls*
>
> *The Swatantra Party stands for the protection of the individual citizen against the increasing trespasses of the State... It is founded on the conviction that social justice and welfare can be attained through the fostering of individual interest and individual*

> *enterprise in all fields better than through State ownership and government control... The Swatantra Party is founded on the claim that individual citizens should be free to hold their property and carry on their professions freely.*

The Swatantra Party was short lived, however, and liberals would have to wait until 1991 when the economy would be liberalised and Indians would finally win economic freedom. Despite the dramatic improvement in the standard of living of millions after the reforms, however, the Indian people have still not converted mentally to the market economy. Reforming politicians are still forced to reform by stealth.

The liberal struggle continues

From the 1970s onwards, the energy of liberals in India turned to social reform and women's rights, where they went on to achieve a number of victories. They continued to follow, by and large, the inspiring vision of an inclusive, democratic and open-minded India nurtured by Gandhi, Nehru and Ambedkar. This vision survived the tragedies of Partition, the lunacy of the License Raj, and the horrors of Indira Gandhi's Emergency. New challenges to liberalism, however, have emerged with the rise of Hindu nationalism. The ideological struggles continue, and a liberal must cope with issues such as these: Does reverse discrimination via caste reservations weaken individual rights? What is the price of free speech when it alienates religious minorities? Why should selling beef kebabs on the street hurt anyone? Why should nationalism have to be only about power? Why should a Hindu feel defensive in a majority Hindu country? I shall discuss these and related issues in the next two chapters.

One of the great achievements of independent India is that, for the most part, we widely condemn discrimination of any kind. We have accepted reservations as compensation in order to lift Dalits and other 'backward' castes, even if many people of the historically privileged castes call it reverse discrimination. As a result of democracy, the oppressed castes have acquired political power through aggressive caste parties. At the same time, we have not undermined the imperative to build talent; hence, we don't envy our software millionaires, who have risen through ability and hard work. This social contract of equity and excellence is something to be proud of.

But the ideology of liberalism, unfortunately, remains an elite enterprise. None of the political leaders of independent

India has managed to build upon Gandhi's remarkable success in pre-Independence India in converting and inspiring the masses with liberal ideas. There is thus a backlash and revulsion against liberals today. They are scorned by Hindu nationalists and as well by leaders of other mass parties for being out of touch with the needs of real people.

5

The Making of an Indian Liberal

In which I recount the journey of my life: from socialism to libertarianism and back to classical liberalism. On the way, I pause at 28 milestones, where I encounter liberal awakenings, lessons and dilemmas. My odyssey, it turns out, is also the story of a nation's struggle to become a liberal democracy.

I am at heart an old-fashioned liberal, the kind that mushroomed in the towns of India in the 19th century. I instinctively believe in democracy and the market, but I realise the need to tame them both, for in their worst form they are a threat to liberty and well-being. My belief in liberalism has been guided by a desire for an ethical, predictable order, a dharma compass, enabling human progress, while protecting the ordinary individual against excessive state or market power. My liberalism is informed by a quiet toleration for all beliefs in a maddeningly diverse country where all paths seem to lead to the same divine unity.

How I got here is the story of this chapter. I recount the ideological journey of my life; from socialism to liberalism, libertarianism and back to classical liberalism. On the way, I pause at 28 milestones, moments where I encountered liberal awakenings, lessons and dilemmas. One of the peak moments was a conversion: Milestone 11 recounts how I became a victim of Nehru's License Raj and responded by switching from a socialist to a libertarian and joined the Swatantra Party. My favourite is at Milestone 26, when the liberal has matured; he responds to another person with a belief opposite to his with an open heart, mutual respect and an ability to appreciate the best quality in her belief. I offer it as the way to live.

My odyssey is also the story of a nation's struggle to become a liberal democracy.

'We Are Actually Free!'

MILESTONE 1: LAHORE, 15 AUGUST 1947

The story begins on the 15th of August 1947, when a five-year-old boy awakens politically. I am that boy. All morning, my mother has been repeating over and over, 'We are free!' Later that day, she tells a visitor that she still can't believe that we are actually free. She has to pinch herself, she says, to be sure she is not dreaming. The wise visitor explains to her that for thousands of years life in India was about power, privilege and oppression. All that has changed, he says. From today, our rulers will only rule us based on our *consent*. The five-year-old doesn't comprehend what the visitor is talking about.

Later, when I grow up, I will understand the meaning of 'consent'. To live in a free republic means that *I* will decide who is to rule over me, and this is the moral basis of a liberal state. It is the first milestone in the making of a middle-class Indian liberal.

~

'Shut the Window!'

MILESTONE 2: JALANDHAR STATION, 25 AUGUST 1947

Our happiness is fleeting, however. Since Britain means to cut us up into two, there is only one question on everyone's mind in the Punjab: Where will my town go—India or Pakistan? A London barrister, Sir Cyril Radcliffe, who has never been to India, has been doing the actual carving on a map over the past six weeks. On 17th August, we learn that Mr Radcliffe has awarded Lahore to Pakistan, and we have become refugees. It is no longer safe to be a Hindu in Pakistan. There is a smell of fear on Lahore's streets as Muslim mobs begin a serious hunt for Hindus and Sikhs. Columns of black smoke are rising from Anarkali Bazaar, which has lost all interest in commerce. The barbers of Lahore are doing brisk business as Sikhs sneak out to get their hair cut, hoping to become inconspicuous and save themselves.

Fortunately, we manage to flee in a military truck, thanks to my uncle, an army major. On the way to the Wagah border, there are caravans of tens of thousands of Hindu refugees walking to India. When we cross the border, my father, my military uncle and our driver give a cheer. We are safe. My mother smiles for the first time in days.

A few days later, we are waiting for the train to move at Jalandhar station on the second leg of our journey. From the window, I see a handsome Muslim policeman, standing tall on duty. All of a sudden, two Sikh teenaged boys emerge from nowhere. Shouting 'Musalman', they thrust their kirpans into the policeman from behind. He does not cry, just falls and dies. Shouting 'Shut the window!' my mother pulls me away.

The five-year-old cannot make sense of the policeman's murder—only one amongst half a million lives lost during the Partition when 20 million Hindus came into India and 18 million Muslims went the other way to Pakistan. The murder introduces me early to the madness lurking in religious crowds, and the modern idea of the absurd.

That terrible moment at Jalandhar station plants the seed of a second liberal idea in my young mind. It will grow with the years; I will realise that insanity is intoxicating, and then it destroys you. Flirting with madness is one thing but madness soon starts flirting with you and then it's too late. It leaves me forever suspicious of religion in the public space, teaching me that faith is not a sound basis for nationhood.

~

The Age of Hope

MILESTONE 3: BHAKRA DAM, 1952

The nightmare of the Partition is a faded memory now. I am growing up in Nehru's free, hopeful India. We are living in the wilds of Bhakra-Nangal, where my engineer father is helping to harness the energy released from dropping an awesome body of water from a 200-metre-high concrete wall stretching half a kilometre across a jagged Himalayan gorge. The great Bhakra Dam inspires feelings bordering on ecstasy among the men working on it.

One fine, ringing morning in 1952, I find myself sitting proudly next to my father. We are listening with reverence to Pandit Nehru speak of the dam as a 'temple of new India'. Probably nowhere, he says, is there a dam as high, where men work tirelessly for the good of mankind. His vision of India is to build a just, casteless, socialist society without the inequalities of wealth. But he wants to do it with democratic freedoms, unlike communist Russia and China. I am inspired by his socialist ideology.

I grow up believing in socialism—in its promise of freedom and equity—not unlike almost everyone else in India and much of the world. It will be some years before I see its dark side.

~

I Fail to Catch the Garland

MILESTONE 4: NEW DELHI, 1954

I am 11, and in Modern School, Delhi. Our class is preparing for United Nations Day. We are marching in single file, learning to salute, turning about face and standing at ease.

The day arrives. India Gate wears a festive look with thousands of students and a continuous stream of flags—the blue UN flag alternating with the Tricolour. We are standing along Rajpath to cheer as the prime minister's motorcade will pass by, going from India Gate to Raisina Hill. There is great excitement—our teacher is hysterical. Pandit Nehru's open car arrives on time, preceded by motorcycles and a pilot car with a siren. He looks unbelievably handsome in a long white coat and cap, a red rose in the lapel. All of a sudden, he throws a garland of marigolds. It comes towards me but I fail to catch it. Brushing my arm, it lands on my neighbour, who becomes an instant celebrity. I am sad, disappointed.

The garland symbolised all the fine things that Nehru gave India: uniting a diverse people into one nation; teaching a love for democracy; nurturing secularism and a respect for minorities; and injecting a scientific spirit with modernist ideals. My failure to catch it was an omen—a prophesy that I would one day turn against Nehru's grand but flawed command socialism that would end up sacrificing growth opportunities for two generations.

I like to see this as a fourth liberal milestone: a premonition of a lesson I will learn one day—that well-meaning socialists end up illiberal when it comes to 'economic freedom'.

~

'Coloured Boys Not S'posed to Get Too Big for Their Boots'

MILESTONE 5: WASHINGTON, DC, 1955

In the mid-1950s, my father is transferred to Washington, DC where the World Bank is mediating the Indus Waters Treaty between India and Pakistan. While he sits down with a red pencil and a map of Punjab with Pakistani engineers to divide the waters of our rivers, I begin high school.

Mistakenly, they have put me in a 'vocational' section, where I am way ahead of my class. My mother pleads with the vice-principal to let me join the 'college prep' section.

He looks at my brown skin, and refuses. Leaning back in his swivel chair, he says in a southern drawl, 'Coloured boys not s'posed to get too big for their boots out here! If you stay out of trouble, you'll graduate after four years with a certificate and a factory job. Welcome to the American dream, son!' It is a moment of political awakening. I have discovered race. America is preaching integration but practising segregation.

I attend a class called 'shop', where I learn to work with my hands—unclog a sink, fix a radio, make a table. That sort of work, my mother says, is meant for the lower castes in India. 'Why are you doing it?' she wails.

It is another political awakening. For the first time I become aware of our caste system back home. Suddenly, I remember the *bhangi* in my grandparents' home, carrying a basketful of shit on his head before they put in a flush system. Middle-class families tend to gloss over caste. I've come to America to discover caste in India. Although American and Indian constitutions state that 'all men are created equal', Blacks and Dalits are not fully human.

It's a different story when a White girl invites me to her integrated birthday party. After the eats, we sit down in a circle to play a game called 'spin the bottle'. One player spins a bottle; when it stops, he gets to kiss the person of the opposite sex in the direction where the bottle points. I find, however, Black boys kissing only Black girls and White boys kissing only White girls. When it comes to my turn, everyone is confused. No one is sure what I, the 'brownie', will do. I quickly solve the problem: I kiss every girl, Black and White. I get to kiss them so often, that I keep getting bonus turns.

Like many American kids, I get a job delivering newspapers before school. Each morning, I go from house to house distributing the *Washington Post.* I have to get up at five a.m., and in the freezing winter this needs a lot of willpower. But my customers depend on me. When it rains or snows, I learn to cover the papers so that people won't have to struggle with wet pages. I have to hold my tongue when they don't pay me on time. My paper route teaches me that the customer is the most important person in America. It is my introduction to the economic side of liberalism—I have become a distributor in the free market economy.

Bounteous liberal awakenings in America, relating to equality, open-mindedness, and free enterprise!

~

A Liberal Education Goes into the Making of a Liberal

MILESTONE 6: HARVARD COLLEGE, 1959

While I am waiting to catch a flight to the US at Palam airport in Delhi, my mother has tears in her eyes, and she is advising me to study something useful at Harvard. 'Why don't you become an engineer like your father? You'll be sure to get a job.' On arriving at Harvard, I try to follow her advice but I discover that my roommate is reading *Anna Karenina* in his Russian Lit class while I'm cramming Bernoulli's equation in fluid mechanics. Over dinner, he says if he were to have an affair with a married woman, it would be with Anna. While he is dreaming of sleeping with Anna Karenina, I'm calculating pipe friction. So, I decide promptly to forget my mother's advice. Before I know it, I am taking courses in Greek tragedy, Sanskrit love poetry, Renaissance painting, Bauhaus architecture, Beethoven's music, the comic spirit, economic history, Plato and Aristotle, and more.

When my mother discovers I am studying Sanskrit, she wails, 'A dead language...only the dead will give him a job!' My father consoles her, saying, 'Education is not only about making a living, it is about making a life. Your son is making a life.'

I went to Harvard to become an engineer but I came out four years later with a degree in philosophy. Without realising it, I had followed my father's maxim—I had 'made a life' among books. Liberal comes from the Latin *liber*, 'free', and the liberal education freed me from authority and expectations, teaching me to question, to think for myself, to depend on my own judgement.

A liberal education will prove decisive in the making of this Indian liberal.

~

I Learn Liberalism from Rawls and Berlin

MILESTONE 7: HARVARD COLLEGE, 1961-63

By the middle of my third year, even liberal Harvard gets worried seeing me flit from course to course. The Dean insists I choose a 'major' and stick to it till graduation. I choose philosophy. Why? Because I want to learn to be happy. John Rawls is the new god of moral and political philosophy and I enrol in his course.

On the first morning he asks us to play a thought game: we are rational, free, self-interested persons in an original position, trying to decide how to order our society.

Neither do we know our class or status, nor our abilities. Rawls claims we will agree to two principles of justice. The first principle guarantees each one the greatest liberty compatible with the same liberty for all. The second posits that equality will be the norm, unless inequality makes the worst-off member better off, and that there will be equality of opportunity as positions and offices in society will be open to all.

To make sense of Rawls's second principle, I try and picture an imaginary CEO who has just delivered huge profits for his company. As a result, his earnings rise to become 50 times that of the lowest paid employee. But everyone else in the company also sees his or her salary rise by 50%. The point being that the lowest paid employee does not grudge the CEO earning far more because his own lot keeps improving. Moreover, there exists equality of opportunity in the company since promotions are given strictly based on results. Thus, everyone in the company can hope to rise upwards. This thought game helps me to understand under what conditions inequality would be fair and acceptable to all in the capitalist system. It would become the centrepiece of Rawls's famous book, *A Theory of Justice*. Over the next 18 months, Rawls introduces me to the basic ideas of liberalism, building on readings of

Locke, Kant, Hume, Mill and others. I go on to write my senior thesis under him, and grow to admire his modest, saintly character.

Visiting Harvard in my final year was Isaiah Berlin, a liberal historian of ideas from Oxford, who was sceptical of all ideologies. Based on a single idea, ideologies, he felt, created unattainable aspirations for a perfect society. Those who got in the way were eggs to be broken while making an omelet. Complete liberty and equality were impossible dreams. Marx's utopia of an equal society had bred a monstrous governing class in the Soviet Union. And if people were also completely free, wolves would eat the sheep. Berlin was especially wary of the violence unleashed by the ideologies of religion—the Crusades, the Spanish Inquisition. I was reminded of India's Partition and I tried to imagine a world without religion.

Liberalism, of course, is also an ideology. But unlike others it is open and is not based on a single big idea. It was the reigning ideology during my Harvard days, and it shook my faith in socialism.

~

Inspired by 'The Mouse Merchant'

MILESTONE 8: CHANDIGARH, 1963

I'm back home for the summer, waiting to go on to Oxford to do a DPhil in philosophy. Lying lazily in a park, I ask myself one evening: Do I really want to spend the rest of my life at that stratosphere of abstract thought? No, I decide I want a life of action. I inform Oxford that I am not coming, and my mother's worst nightmare has come true—she has an unemployed son at home. As news of my idleness spreads, suggestions pour in. A family friend gives me a translation of a thousand-year-old Sanskrit storybook, *Kathasaritsagara,* and tells me to read the story called 'The Mouse Merchant'.

The hero of the story is a poor kid whose father died before he was born, and his mother cleans houses for a living. When the boy grows up, she tells him to go and ask a wealthy merchant in town for advice. While waiting outside the merchant's mansion, the hero sees a dead mouse in his courtyard. When the merchant appears, he asks if he can have the mouse. 'Is that all you want?' the merchant laughs. The boy nods, picks up the mouse, and sells it as cat food to a widow. With the few *paise* he earns, he buys spiced *chana,* which he makes into snack packets. With a pot of water and snacks, he goes and sits at the city's crossroads.

In the afternoon, loggers arrive from the forest. They put down their load and rest. The boy offers each a snack packet and water. Since they have no money, they repay his kindness with a log. The next day he sells a log, buys better snacks, and repeats the same routine. He does this for the next three months till the monsoons arrive. The logging stops; the price of timber shoots up. The young man has a houseful of logs, which he begins to unload in the market. By the end of the season, he has made enough money to buy a shop in the timber market. His competitive advantage lies in his friendship with the loggers; they prefer to deal with him. Before long, he has become a successful timber merchant.

But he is not satisfied, having discovered that building ships from timber is more profitable than timber trading. He finds a ship builder and persuades him to become his partner. Soon, his ship-building business becomes a success. As days go by, he learns that shipping companies earn higher margins than ship builders. Again, he finds a shipper in distress, provides him with capital and before long he's running a successful shipping line. By now, he has become the richest man in town. He asks a jeweller to make him a gold mouse, which he goes and presents to the same rich merchant who had got him started with a dead mouse. The older man is so happy to hear this entrepreneurial tale that he gives his daughter in marriage to our hero.

I am so inspired by this story of India's first start-up that I decide to try my hand at business. I answer the first ad I find in the newspaper, and land a job with Richardson Hindustan Limited in Bombay, selling Vicks VapoRub.

~

I Learn Respect for Bombay's Enterprising Spirit

MILESTONE 9: BOMBAY, SEPTEMBER 1963

I arrive in Bombay on a wet monsoon evening in search of gold and glory. One evening, as I'm walking home, I'm stopped by two women quarrelling. One of them, Munna Bai, complains that the other one is trying to usurp her spot on the pavement. She's been sleeping there since she arrived in the city six months ago. I ask her a dozen questions: What is she doing here? Why did she choose this hard life? Wouldn't she rather be at home with her family in the comfort of her village?

Her reply demolishes me. Picking up a handful of dust

from the earth, she says, 'Sah'b, this is heaven!' I look at her attractive oval face, straight nose and intense eyes. Bombay has given her a job and freedom. In her village in Bihar, she had neither, and she was ceaselessly preyed upon by upper-caste men. Munna Bai gives me new respect for the city. Bombay's capitalism creates jobs, opportunity, and freedom for persons like Munna Bai and me. I realise I too am a migrant like Munna Bai.

Bombay's origins are in commerce, which teaches interdependence: everyone has a customer. The supplier and customer have to be satisfied for the transaction to go through. No one can afford to lord it over another—even Mr Tata has to be nice to his customer. As I metamorphose from a high-thinking brahmin to a money-making bania, I learn from Munna Bai a respect for the big city's enterprise. Another liberal awakening!

~

A Democracy Is Best Run by Modest Persons

MILESTONE 10: 27 MAY 1964-11 JANUARY 1966

Jawaharlal Nehru dies on 27 May 1964. The news arrives on the radio at lunch time and the nation is plunged in grief. There is anxiety, the same question on everyone's lips: 'After Nehru, what?' The foreign press raises alarms of upheaval, including the nation's breakup. It is our first test at leadership succession.

Two weeks later, India is greeted with a smooth, painless and mature transition of power to Lal Bahadur Shastri. We've passed the test. The contrast between Shastri and Nehru is dramatic. Nehru was handsome, aristocratic, charismatic and imperious. His successor is common, diminutive and humble. He looks like a village bumpkin in his dhoti. Nehru was the 'last Englishman to rule India,' combining the English upper-class bias against business with his Kashmiri Brahmin's prejudice against the trading Vaishya. Add to it a strong dose of Fabian socialism at Cambridge, and you have the key to Nehru's economic ideology.

Shastri's gentle face and his kind, large eyes quickly win the nation's affection. But there is more to him. He is pragmatic, not an ideologue, and soon he begins to undo some of the damage of Nehru's socialism. Unlike the latter's obsession with state-owned heavy industry, Shastri returns the nation's attention to agriculture and lays the foundation for a green revolution.

At five feet, two inches, Shastri is pintsize compared to Field Marshall Ayub Khan of Pakistan, who equates puniness with cowardliness and launches an attack in

1965 on Kashmir. The little Indian counters with an efficient attack on Lahore. India has the clear upper hand when ceasefire is declared three weeks later. But Shastri dies of a heart attack in Tashkent while signing the peace treaty. He dies almost penniless—his only possession a second-hand car for which he was still paying instalments.

Some knowledgeable persons who worked with Shastri say that he made a few quiet moves in the direction of liberalising industry as well. Unfortunately, he died before they could be implemented. Had he lived, India's liberalisation might have begun in the 1960s rather than in the 1990s. If that is true, India would have been a different country. But this is speculation, one of those tantalising 'what ifs' of history.

In the nation's history, Nehru is a well-deserved giant. Shastri is almost forgotten. Nehru nurtured democratic institutions, and this was his great gift. He bequeathed to the nation a love for democracy and made Shastri's succession possible. The lesson for a liberal in the making was that institutions matter more than leaders. If good institutions exist, then democracy does not need imperious leaders. It is best run by modest persons like Shastri.

~

A Victim of the Licence Raj

MILESTONE 11: BOMBAY/DELHI, 1968

There is a flu epidemic in 1968, and sales of Vicks go through the roof. At the season's end a summons arrives from Delhi. The company has broken the law—sales have exceeded the authorised, licensed production limit. There is a potential jail sentence. Since my boss is away to America, I attend a hearing in Delhi where the officer treats me like a criminal. I explain that the flu epidemic resulted in extra demand; we only did our duty, keeping pharmacy shelves stocked, helping millions of mothers of children suffering from the flu. If anything, not doing this would have been a crime. But the official pronounces me guilty, and says the law will now take its course. As I'm leaving, I remind the officer to imagine how our country will look in the eyes of the world when national and international newspapers report that our government has sent an executive to jail for alleviating the misery of millions of children during an epidemic. The government quietly drops the enquiry. But as a result of sleepless nights, I've become deeply suspicious of the power of the state and its functionaries.

Well-intentioned Nehru wanted socialism but he created statism, and his command economy snatched away our economic freedom. I was one of its victims. Although no one went to jail in my case, my experience with the government official had a profound impact on my life. I abandoned socialism and became a laissez-faire libertarian, believing in a minimal state.

~

I Join the Swatantra Party

MILESTONE 12: BOMBAY, 1968

I run into the ample, high-spirited Piloo Mody, one of the first members of the Swatantra Party, at a friend's home. He keeps referring to Nehru's 'mixed economy' as a 'mixed-up economy.' By the end of the evening, we've become friends and he invites me to join his study group on economic freedom. We are an eager, motley bunch that meets Friday evenings near Regal Cinema to discuss the theory and practice of the free market. Our group includes the scion of a princely family from Gujarat—I envy him for his striking red Standard Herald sports car. Also in the group are a passionate South Indian executive with a sugar company, several lawyers and an earnest accountant. We read selections from Hayek, Adam Smith,

Locke, J.S. Mill—the greats of classical liberalism, which is the ideology of the Swatantra Party. We meet on Friday evening to discuss and compare what we have read to the current events in India. Minoo Masani, general secretary of the Swatantra Party, pops in occasionally from his office nearby in the Army & Navy building. He is a cold fish, unlike the warm and voluble Piloo. Once, the glamorous Maharani Gayatri Devi of Jaipur drops in, and we can't get over her for weeks.

Disillusioned with socialism, I officially join the Swatantra Party. I am drawn to these words in its manifesto:

> *The Party holds that progress, welfare and happiness of the people depend on individual initiative, enterprise, and energy. The Party stands for the principle of maximum freedom for the individual and minimum interference by the State, consistent with the obligation to prevent and punish anti-social activities, to protect the weaker elements of society, and to create the conditions in which individual initiative will thrive and be fruitful. The Party is, therefore, opposed to increasing State interference of the kind now being pursued.*

Chakravarti Rajagopalachari, better known as Raja-ji, founded the Swatantra Party in 1959. He too makes a cameo appearance in one of our Friday gatherings, reminding us that classical liberalism created America, the first modern country. I am moved by his words as he reads from his essay, 'Have We Lost Our Will to Be Free?':

> *Controlled production, controlled prices and other controls lead to controlling of persons... Happiness, even mere physical happiness, requires not only food, clothing and shelter; but also a sense of freedom. A shortage or total deprivation of any of these essentials makes men and women unhappy. Whether the rope that strangles human beings is made in England or elsewhere or is of indigenous make, makes no difference.*

~

A Liberal Lesson from the Birth of Bangladesh

MILESTONE 13: 1968-1975

After Shastri dies, the old guard of the Congress Party props up Nehru's daughter, Indira Gandhi, thinking she'll be pliable. She turns out to be the opposite—an 'iron lady', who understands power far better than they do. She goes on to become popular with the masses with the slogan *Garibi hatao*, 'Remove poverty'. In the 1971 elections, she wipes out both the old guard of her party and the Opposition, including the Swatantra Party. Later that year, she splits Pakistan into two.

Pakistan, of course, had it coming. Its problems began when Jinnah imposed Urdu, an alien language, on the proud Bengali people of East Pakistan. This was the seed that grew into a movement for secession. When Pakistani generals unleash genocide in late 1971 to stop East Pakistan from seceding, millions of refugees flee into India. Indira Gandhi is forced to intervene, and in two weeks, Indians defeat the Pakistanis, and a new state of Bangladesh is born.

It is a cautionary tale for arrogant, illiberal leaders who impose majoritarian whims on their people. Sri Lanka makes the same mistake, imposing Sinhala language and exclusive cultural ideas on the Tamils. As a result, the island nation will lose a generation in a horrific civil war. Independent India may have made many mistakes through the second half of the 20th century, but language chauvinism is not one of them. Although Hindi nationalists tried to impose Hindi on the rest of India, they backed off quickly when the Tamils threatened to secede.

The liberal in me is also troubled by Indira Gandhi's

sharp turn to the left. Guided by a Marxist coterie, she has aligned with Soviet Russia, and begun nationalising banks, insurance, coal, steel companies, and more. She tries to nationalise the trade in food grains, but has to back off, realising the disaster she has created. She brings more socialist controls on the private sector. Although it was her father who established the 'license raj', I find it difficult to blame him—he was the product of a socialist age. But I squarely blame Indira Gandhi for not changing course when Japan, Korea and Taiwan have shown the way. Their success lies in opening their economies, adopting export-oriented policies, while India persists with a closed economy, wallowing in export pessimism. These nations go on to become 'Asian Tigers' while Indira's India remains a closed, command economy that is suppressing growth, keeping the nation poor, to become one of the worst performing in the world.

There are lessons for a liberal here. One, the state should not impose a language or culture on a people. Two, the state is meant to govern, not run business enterprises.

~

'Indira Is India, India Is Indira'

MILESTONE 14: 25 JUNE 1975-21 MARCH 1977

I come home early one evening and announce to my family that the Allahabad High Court has found Indira Gandhi guilty of corruption—of misusing the services of government officials during her election campaign. It seems to be an impropriety, not a grave offence that could disqualify her from holding office. Moreover, she has won her seat by 100,000 votes. But the judge has taken a tough stand.

Instead of resigning, Mrs G declares a 'state of emergency', suspending constitutional freedoms. Before dawn, the police wake up political opponents and lock them up. In the next thirty-six hours, India changes from a democracy to an autocracy. The number of political opponents in jail soon climbs to 100,000 persons.

Mrs G trusts only her younger son, Sanjay Gandhi, and power thus shifts to him. He lets loose a reign of terror. One of his pet projects is population control. He hits upon the idea of sterilising men—anyone with more than two children is to be vasectomised. With monthly quotas to fulfil, petty officials scramble to catch any male in sight, young or old. A reporter in Bihar finds only women in the bazaar, the men have all run away, afraid they will end up on an operating table, their genitals cut off. The drive will eventually sterilise 6.2 million men.

No one knows quite what is happening. Newspapers are full of blank spaces because the censor has stopped a story at the last minute. Or there is a recipe for cucumber raita on the front page that a more creative censor has substituted for an inconvenient story. The first thing dictators do is to finish off the press. The mother and son do exactly that. It doesn't seem to take much effort. The press bows to the tyrant's will—L.K. Advani of the Bharatiya Jan Sangh (which would later become the Bharatiya Janata Janata Party [BJP]), chastises the press: 'You were asked to bend, but you crawled.'

Mrs G claims she has saved India from anarchy, from opposition leaders like Jayaprakash Narayan, who she says are all funded by a 'foreign hand'. Unafraid, my friend Piloo Mody walks into the parliament with a placard that reads: 'I'm a CIA Agent'. Mrs G is not amused and throws him in jail. In a dictatorship, there is never any dearth of willing slaves. The Congress President, D.K. Barooah, proclaims, 'Indira is India, India is Indira'. Meanwhile, some of my friends celebrate: 'How wonderful! The trains are running on time, everyone is working, the streets are clean.'

In the end, Mrs G calls a hurried election and loses. Why does the dictator make this rash mistake? A deeply insecure woman, she wants to be loved. Her sycophants tell her she is the darling of the masses, and predict a landslide victory. Common sense should have told her that mass sterilisation was evil and idiotic. Dictators are never as strong as they imagine and people never as weak as they think. The nation's spine does not bend. Luckily, the illiberal nightmare lasts only 21 months and democracy is restored in the end. It was India's darkest, most illiberal moment. Ironically, it was the suppressing of free expression and other liberal freedoms, which Mrs G was convinced would strengthen her rule, that eventually led to the dictator's downfall.

~

When Pushed to the Wall, You'll Try Anything

MILESTONE 15: BOMBAY/DELHI, 1980

I am now 37 and CEO of Richardson Hindustan Ltd, the company where I started almost at the bottom. But I'm not happy. Our company is in serious trouble. The government has decreed a severe price control on medicines that threatens to bankrupt us.

Fortunately, I have an inventive team. In the midst of a gloomy morning meeting, our creative Gujarati head of marketing wonders, 'What if Vicks VapoRub had been an Ayurvedic, not a Western drug?' The others snicker, thinking it a joke. Behind the 'what if' is a hope—Ayurvedic medicines are apparently not under price control. The Tamil head of R&D adds to the speculative thought game. 'Well, VapoRub's ingredients *are* natural.' The Marwari company secretary says that he will check if, indeed, Ayurvedics are price-control free. The Punjabi sales manager, sensing an opportunity, informs the team that unlike Western medicines, the distribution of Ayurvedics is not limited to drug stores. His imagination is running wild with visions of Vicks becoming available in millions of corner stores across the country. The Bengali finance manager pours cold water over these wondrous imaginings. He cautions us that even if turns out that VapoRub's ingredients are in the Ayurvedic formulary, it would be illegal to make the switch. Would the government ever allow it? The wishful Gujarati, who'd started the thought game, announces a headline in the *Times of India*: 'A 100-year-old American product becomes a 2000-year-old Indian medicine!' Everyone has a laugh.

The team members know, however, exactly what to do. The R&D man rushes to check if VapoRub's ingredients are in the Ayurvedic formulary. The finance manager heads off to our lawyer's office to confirm if Ayurvedics are indeed price-control free. The company secretary asks our Delhi office if and how VapoRub's registration could be changed. The sales manager goes to the bazaar to find out where Ayurvedics are sold. In the evening the team reconvenes. There are smiling faces all around. The answer is 'yes' on all counts. We look at each other in disbelief.

When our application lands on his desk, the regulator practically falls off his chair. He guesses what we are up to but he can't stop us—it is all perfectly legal. Six weeks later, shiny bottles of 'All natural Ayurvedic Vicks VapoRub' are sitting proudly on store shelves. In six months, the stores carrying Vicks jump from 60,000 pharmacies to 750,000 general stores. Nothing has changed, except our profits. The company survives, thanks to a speculative thought game and excellent teamwork.

One of liberalism's prized values is open-mindedness. It is this openness of spirit that morning which brought out the best in our team, making us think laterally and adopt the Indian ideal of *jugaad*, making it possible for us to innovate on the fly. The end result was that the company's profits were restored to a degree that some of the surplus profits could be invested in an R&D centre to investigate

Ayurvedic medicines according to the protocols of modern science in order to prove their efficacy and safety, and take them to consumers around the world.

~

If Greed Is the Flaw of Capitalism, Envy Is the Sin of Socialism

MILESTONE 16: MOSCOW, 1989

In the mid-1980s, Procter & Gamble Co, the American consumer products giant, buys Richardson Vicks, our parent company worldwide, and overnight we become Procter & Gamble India. It is also the time when the Soviet Union is facing severe shortages. It has no dollars and is unable to import anything from the West. It has rupees, however, because of a lively rupee-rouble trade. Many Indian companies step in to fill the gap. We are one of them. The Russians place a sizeable order for Crest toothpaste, and I decide to visit Moscow to explore further opportunities.

My first impression of the USSR is of amazing equality. But I am shocked to find the stores are empty and people look grim. Everyone seems to be an employee of the state, including my taxi driver. No one, however, seems to want to work. The driver refuses to take me to my next appointment unless I give him a bribe. He is a chatter box, and is envious of my briefcase, my leather shoes and my sun glasses.

By creating equality, socialism was supposed to eliminate human envy. I realise that as levelling increases in society, envy also rises. In a capitalist society, the difference between a billionaire and a taxi driver is too great for the latter to feel envy for the former. Envy pervades the Soviet Union because the differences are tiny. It doesn't make sense to envy the Queen of England, but if my neighbour discovers that I have come into possession of a beautiful tablecloth, she feels envious. Near equals feel envy. If greed is the flaw of capitalism, envy is the sin of socialism. John Rawls, my teacher, used to say, 'A person who envies another is prepared to make both persons worse off to reduce the gap between them.'

I believe there is a moral case for equality. It is natural to feel compassion for those not favoured by nature. Many of us want to compensate those who have lost out in nature's lottery or have suffered from undeserved bad luck—for being born dull, for having bad parents, for having disagreeable personalities, accidents and illnesses. In modern democracies, the left's answer is to have an extensive welfare state, and thereby diminish inequality. The right is suspicious of egalitarianism because the impulse for equality can curb liberty, as it did in the Soviet Union and in all communist states.

Neither the left nor the right would quarrel with a just society in which inequalities are perceived to be fair and deserved. To achieve this, John Rawls came up with an elegant answer. What if the advantages of the better off could help to improve the chances of the worst off? Then, there might be fewer reasons to envy. Recall the thought game of the imaginary CEO that I recounted at Milestone 7 earlier in this chapter. The left looks to the state as a great insurance company, which takes from people who have succeeded to compensate those who failed. But I believe that the sustainable answer is to try and create equality of opportunity. Hence, I tend to focus on improving schools and healthcare for all citizens, and especially the poor. This is not easy to achieve. Despite having excellent schools and healthcare, no one seems to have found a way to compensate for backgrounds and uneven home influences.

My visit to the Soviet Union convinced me that absolute equality is unachievable because the human ego will not shrink that far. The best one can hope for is fair inequality. If people believe that an inequality is fair, then they are more likely to accept it. For example, people are more likely to accept inequalities that result from hard work and talent rather than luck or privilege. If the rich pay their taxes, create mass employment, generate significant wealth for a nation, the inequality of their situation is more likely to be accepted as just.

~

The End of History

MILESTONE 17: BERLIN, 1989; USSR, 1991

A few months after I return from Moscow, the Berlin Wall falls. Dividing East and West Berlin, it had symbolised the division between communist Eastern Europe and capitalist Western Europe. Its fall on 9 November 1989 marks a pivotal moment in world history. Peaceful revolutions soon follow in other Eastern European countries, leading to the end of communist rule. In East Germany, Hungary, Czechoslovakia, Poland and others, communist governments are replaced by democratic and market-oriented systems, and this sets the stage for the dissolution of the Soviet Union in 1991. Thus ends the Cold War.

Fascism was defeated in the Second World War and

communism is now almost dead. Liberalism has triumphed decisively over its two biggest enemies in the 20th century. This is 'The End of History', proposes a young liberal political scientist, Francis Fukuyama, in an essay, which he later expands into a book, *The End of History and the Last Man* (1992). Fukuyama argues that the fall of communism and the triumph of liberal democracy and market capitalism in the late 20th century represents the 'end point of mankind's ideological evolution', heralding a new world order for the 21st century. Marxists had hoped for the opposite—that a communist utopia would be the end of history. Instead, liberals now hope that liberal democracy will become the legitimate and dominant form of governance because of its superiority in providing political and economic stability, individual freedoms and prosperity.

Fukuyama's thesis becomes an instant hit in the neo-liberal mood of the times. In the Anglosphere, Margaret Thatcher in the UK and Ronald Reagan in the US become its flag-bearers. Indeed, in the 30 years between 1970s and 2000, democracies do expand from 35 to well over a 100. So does market capitalism. In the years that follow, the idea of 'The End of History' will turn out to be a premature triumph. Samuel P. Huntington, another political scientist, publishes *The Clash of Civilizations?* in 1993, which challenges Fukuyama's thesis, offering an alternative vision of the world order. He identifies several major civilisations—Western, Islamic, Confucian, Hindu—and predicts conflicts between them. He feels that cultural fault lines will lead to tensions and clashes, particularly between the West and the Islamic worlds. He will be proved correct on 9/11, 2002.

~

India's Golden Summer of 1991

MILESTONE 18: DELHI, JULY 1991

In the golden summer of 1991, liberalism also triumphed in India, when Indians won their economic freedom after four decades of being shackled by a command economy. The economic reforms would unleash Indian entrepreneurship and go on to transform a stagnant economy into a dynamic one. Indians, however, do not generally connect their pathbreaking liberalisation with the world history narrated in the previous milestone. This is probably because India was from the beginning a democratic country, not an authoritarian, communist regime. Nevertheless, India's turn from state socialism and the command economy of the previous four decades coincided with the liberal revolution that was sweeping the globe, and country after country seemed to be becoming democratic capitalist.

That summer began with a tragedy.

In May 1991, a human bomb kills innocent, idealistic Rajiv Gandhi, India's prime minister. I am especially sad because he was an early reformer. Since no one in the dynasty is ready to take over, the Congress Party chooses 70-year-old Narasimha Rao. He is quiet and dull, and threatens no one. They see him as a 'stop-gap' to head a minority government that no one thinks will last very long. The country, meanwhile is in the midst of an economic crisis. Foreign reserves have depleted dangerously, barely enough to cover three weeks of imports; growth has slowed and inflation is in double digits. Rao's first decision is to get a good finance minister. His choice is I.G. Patel, who has returned recently after heading the London School of Economics. But it does not work out, so he settles for a younger man—a reticent and soft-spoken economist, Manmohan Singh. Rao also brings in a tough, action-oriented principal secretary, Amar Nath Verma, who had championed delicensing in his previous position.

To everyone's surprise, the government quietly

unleashes the biggest revolution in India's economic history, embarking on a bold programme of liberalisation that opens a closed economy to foreign investment and trade, dismantles import controls, virtually abolishes licensing in industry, breaks public sector monopolies, lowers tax rates and customs duties, and devalues the currency. By 1993, foreign exchange reserves shoot up from $1 billion to $20 billion; the economy has begun to grow; inflation has fallen from 13 percent to 6 per cent a year; foreign investment is up thirty-fold; government revenues are growing despite lower tax rates. It is quite an achievement—as important a turning point for India as Deng's revolution in China in December 1978.

Once the crisis is over, the pressure diminishes, the reforms stop. There is no national soul-searching over the failure of the state socialism of Nehru and Indira Gandhi. The commissars of the License Raj quietly become liberalisers. The reformers do not bother to sell the reforms. It is all 'hush hush' for fear of the left, particularly the powerful left wing of the Congress Party. Prime Minister Rao comes under attack by his own party. In the 1996 elections, the people too boot out Rao and the Congress Party. Many influential voices in the party blame the reforms for the loss. It is incredible: this had been India's great moment, and neither Rao, nor the Congress Party, seemed to take credit for saving the country from an economic disaster and setting it on a path of high growth. Why did economic success not translate into political gains?

Even today, thirty years after the reforms, India's political class believes that reforms are a vote loser. No Indian politician bothers to sell the reforms or the competitive market to the public. It is quite unlike Britain, where the passionate reformer, Margaret Thatcher, claimed to spend 20% of her time doing the reforms and 80% selling them. Politicians in India continue to reform hesitantly and by stealth. Since 1991, every government has reformed in a slow, stealthy manner. But even the slow reforms have added up to make India one of the world's fastest growing economies. As a result, around 400 million people have crossed the poverty line and there is a rapidly growing middle class. People can see the tangible, positive impact that the reforms have had on their lives. There were, for example, only 10 million telephones in India before 1991. Today, there are over a billion! But most people do not connect their improved life to the liberal reforms.

Indians continue to believe that the market makes the rich richer and the poor poorer. They cannot distinguish between being pro-market and pro-business, and feel businesses are the main beneficiaries of economic reforms. The lesson for the liberal reformer is that the benefits of the competitive market are not intuitive. It is hard to understand how millions working in their own self-interest can bring prosperity to the whole society. This is why Adam Smith called it an 'invisible hand'. The market has to be sold to the voter in a democracy, who needs to understand that pro-market policies bring greater competition, which improves the quality of products and keeps prices in check, and this helps everyone. No businessman really wants more competition in his field. Thus, there is a difference between being pro-market and pro-business. Ironically, it was discretionary power in bureaucratic hands during the License Raj that permitted officials to dole out favours to individual businesses, which was, in fact, pro-business.

~

The Rise of Hinglish

MILESTONE 19: NORTH INDIA, 1990s

The liberalisation of the nineties sets in motion profound changes across India. The minds of the young become suddenly freer. The new satellite TV channels show what is happening in the world. The growth of industry brings migrants from villages to the cities. In the cities, a new middle class grows, with ambitions for unheard-of careers. IT entrepreneurs become role models, creating an aspiration among the young to start their own businesses.

I uncovered many such liberations during my travels in the nineties and reported them in my book *India Unbound*. The most interesting one was seeing English quietly become an Indian language. Young people, in particular, thought of it as a functional tool to navigate the world, losing thus the fear of having to speak in the right accent. Simultaneously, a curious mixture of English and Hindi arose in the bazaar. They called it 'Hinglish'. Advertising slogans claimed 'Life ho to aisi' and 'Dil mange more'. My newspaper boy assured me, 'Aaj busy hoon, kal bill milega, definitely.' The bania's assistant warned me about the vamp in our neighbourhood: 'Careful Sir-ji, voh dangerous hai!' The Zee News evening bulletin offered a mixture of three English and four Hindi words: 'Aaj Middle East mein peace ho gai!' Linguistic purists were horrified with this mixture, but I thought of it as a liberation. It was a breathable idiom, loose like a saree, not a buttoned-up suit and tie. Indian English had been set free.

Indians had, of course, been mixing English words

with their mother tongues for a hundred years. Earlier, it had been aspirational idiom—a sign of upward mobility in the emerging old middle class. Now Hinglish (and its regional variants) was the 'cool' way to speak even in upper-middle-class drawing rooms. I wondered if Hinglish could become the national language one day. This was how English, in fact, had grown out of an Anglo-Saxon mixture in the bazaar during the 14th century when the upper classes spoke French and the educated clergy spoke Latin. But then Shakespeare came along in a hundred years, borrowing freely from everywhere. Would Hinglish have to wait for its Shakespeare? Salman Rushdie had begun the liberation of Indian English by 'chutnifying' it. But his was not Hinglish, and it came before the great liberation of the nineties when Hinglish became ubiquitous.

As a result of these developments, I no longer worry about being deracinated—the old, colonial disease. I feel a person can be multi-rooted, like a banyan tree. Languages evolve naturally, and one shouldn't get too anxious. After the experience of Pakistan's breakup and Sri Lanka's civil war, the liberal in me certainly does not want the state to interfere, telling us what to speak. The rise of Hinglish and its variants in other regional languages is a liberal moment in the nation's history. It happened at the same time as the economy was being liberalised, leading to the rise of an aspirational, more confident small-town middle class.

~

History Makes a Comeback, Liberalism Retreats

MILESTONE 20: NEW YORK, 9/11 and MUMBAI, 26/11

On the morning of 11 September 2001, 19 Islamic militants of an extremist group, Al Qaeda, hijack four domestic American airline flights and crash two of the planes into the tallest buildings in New York City, and a third into the Pentagon near Washington, DC. The fourth crashes in rural Pennsylvania after a passenger revolts. Nearly 3,000 people die, including the 19 terrorists. It results in a global war on terror led by the United States, which lasts for two decades.

About three months after the 9/11 attack, I am invited by Citibank, New York, to speak about the future of India and emerging markets to its top management team. The invitation comes from the CEO, who has apparently read *India Unbound*. He felt I might have something worthwhile to tell the senior members of his team who were gathering together from around the world for an annual get-together.

First-class tickets from Delhi and a suite in St Regis hotel are part of the temptation. My talk is scheduled for 7 p.m. on a Monday evening. I arrive promptly at 6.30. The receptionist has left, and the building security refuses to let me go up to the top-floor conference room. The guard keeps calling and getting voice mail from both the numbers he is authorised to call. I have only one number and it isn't answered either.

I plead with the head of security, explaining that my invitation has come from the CEO. 'Why don't you call his office?' I urge him. He does not have the CEO's number. I feel frustrated and upset, but I wait patiently. An hour later, feeling defeated, I walk back to the hotel, where there are lots of panicky messages waiting for me. In the end, my hosts are contrite over the mix-up, which was apparently due to new security rules for high-rise buildings instituted after 9/11. The bank, it seems, has recently outsourced its security to a new firm. Neither the firm's employees, nor Citi bankers have quite got the hang of the new situation. I never manage to give my speech because most of the bank's top team leave the following day.

On the flight back to Delhi, I reflect on this bizarre experience. Osama bin Laden, the leader of Al Qaeda, I feel, has won. He has defeated liberal America. Americans are confused, if not in panic. What had been an amazingly open and confident society, has suddenly turned fearful and paranoid. America had always been easy-going about domestic security; now barriers have come up in all sorts of places. The President, George Bush Jr, has vowed revenge against Islamic terror. There are daily reports about upping the security apparatus, intelligence gathering, surveillance and counter-attacks. The easy-going American state has become intrusive.

Seven years later, on the other side of the globe, India becomes the target on a smaller scale of Islamic terror. On 26 November 2008, a group of ten heavily armed terrorists from Pakistan associated with the Lashkar-e-Taiba launch a coordinated attack on Mumbai. The terrorists target multiple locations, including prominent hotels, a railway station, a popular café and a Jewish community centre. They fire indiscriminately on civilians and take hostages during their three-day siege, resulting in the loss of 166 lives and injury to hundreds. The Mumbai attack, which would come to be referred to as 26/11, is the deadliest terrorist incident in Indian history. Unlike the United States, which launches military operations in Afghanistan in response to 9/11, India's response is restrained. It does not vow to exact immediate military revenge on Pakistan, mindful of nuclear arms in both states. It focuses on strengthening security measures, enhancing intelligence capabilities, and pursuing diplomatic solutions.

Fundamentalism is the polar opposite of liberalism. Islamic fundamentalism represents a major threat to liberal values, culture and politics. From an Islamic perspective, the root of the 9/11 attack lay in the perceived wrongs of history perpetrated by Western imperialism in the Islamic world of West Asia. The attacks of 9/11 and the US response represented a retreat of liberalism, cutting short the neoliberal triumph proposed by Fukuyama in 'The End of History'. History had come back.

~

When Secularism Let Us Down

MILESTONE 21: GODHRA,
27 FEBRUARY 2002—ECHOES OF DELHI,
NOVEMBER 1984

It is difficult to speak of the murder of innocent people, but it is also impossible to remain silent.

On the morning of 27 February 2002, a train arrives at Godhra's railway station in Gujarat, filled with Hindu pilgrims returning from Ayodhya. An argument erupts on the platform between passengers and hawkers, and soon turns violent. Suddenly four coaches of the Sabarmati Express are burning, with 59 people trapped inside. They all die in the fire. Riots erupt across Gujarat and continue over the next three days, and there is sporadic violence for a whole year. The death toll in the end is 1,044 Muslims and 254 Hindus, according to official sources. Chief Minister Narendra Modi's BJP state government is accused of failing to control the violence and opposition parties demand the chief minister's resignation.

My worst fears of the Partition return to haunt me as I watch scenes of horror night after night on television. There are no moderate voices, only shrill, harsh ones. What has gone wrong? Secularists blame BJP's electoral strategy of polarising the Hindus to win votes. Hindu nationalists blame the Congress Party's strategy of appealing to Muslim vote banks. Unfortunately, there is no Mahatma Gandhi in 2002 to keep the peace. In 1947, Gandhi had trudged successfully through the Bengal countryside, a one-man peacekeeping force; hence, Bengal had remained relatively peaceful, unlike Punjab. The only words that console me in those terrible weeks and months of 2002 are an odd statement by a European tourist on prime-time TV. In an impromptu interview on a street corner in Mumbai, she says that in a country of a billion people of strong religious emotion, it is remarkable that there has been so little violence in India.

Ever since Partition, India has experienced sporadic incidents of communal violence. I remember vividly the carnage in Delhi in 1984 when one of our company's employees, a Sikh boy, got roughed up. It had happened after Indira Gandhi's murder by her Sikh bodyguards. During the following days, there had been riots all over Delhi in which Hindus had taken revenge and 3,000 Sikhs had died. Later, senior leaders of the Congress Party were implicated for inciting the mobs. Rajiv Gandhi had said, infamously: 'When a big tree falls, the earth shakes.'

On this occasion in Gujarat in 2002, I was equally disappointed with Prime Minister Vajpayee. He had preached the virtues of tolerance, but had failed to act. After all, he had condemned the assault on the Babri Masjid a decade earlier—but he failed on this occasion. I was to learn later that Mr Vajpayee had been extremely upset and had planned to sack Chief Minister Modi at the BJP's national executive meeting in Goa. But Modi pulled the rug from under the prime minister's feet—he surprised everyone at the meeting, offering to resign. There were loud cries of 'No, no!' heard around the room. Arun Shourie, one of Vajpayee's ministers, rose to explain why the Gujarat chief minister should resign. But his voice was drowned by the crowd of Modi's supporters. Mr Vajpayee remained silent, humiliated and outsmarted. It turned out to be a masterstroke by or on Modi's behalf.

It is important to ask ourselves where the excellent idea of secularism failed us. Why couldn't it stem the tide of intolerance? Easy-going Hinduism is tolerance itself. India's Muslims too are amongst the most moderate in the world. Hinduism is a way of life, not a way of belief. It has millions of gods, who coexist peacefully. None of them is a jealous god. Hinduism is quite unlike the Abrahamic religions—it doesn't have one book, nor one prophet. Even an atheist can be a respectable Hindu. Hindus, I believe, are too diverse, too individualistic to accept the monolithic political ideology of Hindutva.

So, what went wrong, both in the riots in Gujarat 2002 and in Delhi in 1984? Why couldn't the Constitutional ideology of liberal secularism prevent the violence? Was it, perhaps, because the most vocal secularists were English-speaking, atheist intellectuals who had contempt for believers? They could see only the dark side of religion, its intolerance, forgetting that religion has given meaning to humanity since the dawn of civilisation. Because secularists spoke a language alien to the vast majority of Indians, they were only able to condemn communal violence, not stop it. There had been no dialogue between the two sides ever since Mahatma Gandhi died.

English-speaking liberals and their siblings behave like members of an exclusive private club, snobbish about their secularism, treating religion not as a way of life but as superstition. It is bad enough that only around 15% of India understands their language, English. The rest feel deaf in their own country. By incessantly parroting secularism, they may have created an empty domain, where ordinary religious persons are lesser human beings. This inability to speak to people partially explains the rise of Hindu nationalism. There are no voices of moderate Hindus or Muslims, only shrill voices of extremists at both ends. Our parents and grandparents used to listen to Mahatma Gandhi, Maulana Azad, Vivekananda, Aurobindo—all steeped in religion, speaking with credibility. Today, the middle ground is empty.

Our intellectual liberals were influenced by 19th-century European thinkers like Nietzsche, who declared famously that God is dead; Feuerbach argued that God was a projection of the human imagination; Durkheim felt religion reflected society, its rituals and sentiments bound people; Freud declared it an illusion which made civilisation possible;

Marx said the illusion originated in the alienation of the capitalist worker for whom religion was like opium, a drug to soothe his pain, and once capitalism was destroyed, the drug wouldn't be needed. Of course, many Indian intellectuals are also familiar with the Indian idea of secularism as *sarva dharma sambhava*, but the inner contempt of an atheist for religion comes through to the believer.

Many liberals think of communal violence as a governance issue—failure of law and order. But surely, it is more. Why did half a million people have to die in the 1947 riots? Why couldn't we prevent that tragedy? We still do not have an answer. Perhaps, it will come from literature one day. Just as Tolstoy's *War and Peace* brought closure to the Russian mind, uneasy from the tragedy of Napoleonic wars. While we wait for our own 'War and Peace', let's remember that communal harmony will not come from weaning people away from religion. It will come when moderate leaders, seeped in religion, raise a public call to privatise religion. It also means rethinking the lofty Indian ideal of secularism, *sarva dharma sambhava*, 'respect for all religions', and adopting the universal liberal ideal of separation of religion and politics. I shall elaborate this further in Chapter 7.

~

I Discover India's Miracle in Tahrir Square

MILESTONE 22: TAHRIR SQUARE, CAIRO, 8 APRIL 2011

On the 8th of April 2011, I am in Cairo, invited by the pro-democracy protest movement of the Arab Spring to speak on the 'Indian model' for Egypt's future. Someone, it seems, has read *India Unbound*, which is why I got a ticket to history in the making. Young Egyptian journalists ask me three pointed questions at the end: (1) How did you keep the generals out of power? (2) How did you become one of the fastest growing economies, and a global outsourcer of IT services? (3) How did you achieve social harmony in the world's most diverse country? In particular, how did India manage to have such a moderate Muslim population?

I'm not sure how well I answered their questions. But they made me think. Clearly, they were the right questions, nailing the three attributes of a successful nation—democracy, prosperity and social harmony. They forced me to relook at my country.

The first question was their way of asking how India had managed to remain democratic over the past 65 years. We were lucky, I feel. The first generation of India's leaders were 'freedom fighters'. Even the army held them in awe.

More than anyone, Jawaharlal Nehru deserves credit for embedding democracy and the rule of law. Although he was not a Gandhi and could not 'sell' the liberal ideals of the Constitution to the masses, as only the Mahatma could, he upheld those ideals against all detractors of liberal institutions.

The answer to the economic question is market-based reforms. After four disastrous decades, India finally got its act together in 1991. Since then, every government has reformed in a slow, stealthy manner, but even slow reforms added up to make India one of the world's most dynamic economies.

The third question of the young Egyptians reflected the Arab Spring's fear of radical Islam. They explained that 12% of Egyptians were Christian and didn't feel secure. At the same time, 14% of Indians were Muslim and they did feel secure. How did this happen? I didn't have a good answer but I felt, then, that India's composite culture, a natural outcome of at least two millennia of diverse people, migrants and ancient residents, had something to do with it. Of course, this situation did change after 2014, so perhaps the answer to that question I was asked back in 2011 is not as simple.

That afternoon in Cairo, the conference is cut short

because a spontaneous protest has erupted next door at Tahrir Square. Having nothing better to do, I wander off to the Square. I can't understand a word they are saying. But before I know it, the host of our conference rushes up to me, urging me to say a few words in three minutes. Soon, I am being pushed through the maddening crowd and lifted on to the stage.

'I bring greetings from Al Hind, the land of Gandhi,' I improvise. The crowd breaks into applause. Clearly, I've made a good start. The translator gives me an encouraging look. I remember the words of my history teacher, and I repeat them: 'Democracy is about people like you and me deciding not to be ruled by the high and mighty. But you will say, I don't know how to rule. I say that it is better to have leaders who don't know how to rule than to have leaders who know how to rule but who are corrupt.' I am now getting into the rhythm and begin to speak about the rule of law. It is a mistake. The crowd quickly loses interest. It is far more concerned with hanging the generals than in learning about the pillars of democracy. My three minutes are also up.

At three o'clock the next morning I wake up to the sound of gunfire. They must be bursting firecrackers, I think. There is a knock on my door in Shepherd Hotel.

It is my host in pyjamas, whispering that the army has moved into Tahrir Square. I should be prepared to flee as my 'three minutes of fame' has been posted on YouTube. Filled with fear, I change quickly, pick up my laptop and passport, and wait on the armchair. I must have fallen asleep. The next thing I know, it is seven o'clock and I am still alive. A thick cloud of smoke can be seen from my window over Tahrir Square. I switch on the TV, turn to Al Jazeera. Yes, the army has come. They have been looking for soldiers and have found two officers hiding in the adjoining mosque. After capturing the officers, they have left quickly. I am still filled with fear. So, I hop on the first flight home. Only when our plane enters Indian airspace do I breathe easy, feeling a new respect for my relatively peaceful, stable country.

Almost thirteen years later, the Arab Spring is long gone. Little seems to have changed in the Middle East. Tunisians replaced their dictator with a democracy, but it is struggling. In Egypt, they replaced one autocratic ruler (Hosni Mubarak) with another (Abdel Fattah el-Sisi). The old elites have regained power. Libya, Syria and Yemen descended into civil war and collapsed. The lesson for a liberal is that a revolution for democracy does not necessarily lead to democracy. The French Revolution, the first such revolution, descended into violence and authoritarianism. The revolutions through Europe in 1848 gave a glimmer of democratic hope before being extinguished. It took Europe a century to fulfil the promise of its uprisings. Democratic transitions require enabling institutions of the state and this can take decades.

The Arab Spring has taught me how difficult it is to embed liberal democracy. I realise that India's case is something of a miracle. Democracy's persistence is exceptional among post-colonial societies. I do not have to look far to see the norm—Pakistan, next door, is 'an army with a country'. Why India succeeded, I can only guess. Andre Malraux was right when he said that the independent Indian nation was founded by saints under the shadows of Hitler, Stalin and Mao. They were our 'liberators with clean hands'. Even Indira Gandhi, the autocrat, could not destroy it.

~

'India Grows at Night When the Government Sleeps'

MILESTONE 23: JANTAR MANTAR, NEW DELHI,
5 APRIL 2011

Around the same time as the Arab Spring, there is a similar uprising in Delhi relating to a crisis in public morality. Corruption scandals have erupted in the Congress-led UPA government, and Anna Hazare, a simple, elderly, straight-talking Gandhian, begins a series of protests, calling on the government to act against spreading corruption. The response to the Anna Andolan surprises everyone, stirring the politically shy urban middle class, bringing youth to the streets. The movement is short lived, however. Its lasting legacy is to give birth to the Aam Aadmi Party led by Arvind Kejriwal, who was Hazare's second-in-command. It also brings down the Congress Party, giving a boost to Narendra Modi of the BJP, who builds his campaign for the 2014 Lok Sabha elections on the promise of fighting corruption.

Ironically, the previous decade, when the UPA was in power, had also been the best in India's economic history. The economy had grown at an average of 7.5 per cent a year while population growth had begun to slow. It was an odd sight to see prosperity spreading amidst corruption and bad governance. India seemed to be rising despite the state. Where the state was desperately needed—in providing basic education, healthcare, law and order, drinking water—it was performing dismally. Where it was not needed, it was still hyperactive in stifling small private enterprises through red tape and the 'inspector raj'. India's was a 'bottom-up' story, unlike China's 'top-down' success that had been orchestrated by an authoritarian state.

India's story of private success and public failure was symbolised by the astonishing rise of Gurgaon, a sleepy village on the outskirts of Delhi. It had risen without a municipality or reasonable public services. But in 25 years, it went on to become home to the world's largest corporations with 32 million square feet of commercial space. It had fabled apartment complexes with swimming pools, spas and saunas, dozens of skyscrapers, over two dozen shopping malls, seven golf courses and countless showrooms of world-famous luxury brands. But it had no reliable public services—the sewage system was undependable; the water supply and electricity were unpredictable, there were few decent roads and virtually no public transport. All the public goods were privately provided. Not having a municipality had meant less red tape, less corruption, fewer bureaucrats to block private enterprise, but there was hardly any public infrastructure.

(To be fair, the state did finally wake up and since then it has done a reasonable job of providing these public goods.)

Seeing the miracle, people of Gurgaon used to ask: Why do we need a government at all with corrupt politicians and unresponsive bureaucrats? Shrugging their shoulders, they declared cynically, 'India grows at night when the government sleeps.' The first part of this statement became the title of one of my books, in which I made a passionate case for better governance. The moral of this tale is not to celebrate modern India's heroic rise despite the state, but the crucial need to reform a weak, ineffective state.

As a result, my political position has also changed. After experiencing the pain of the 'licence raj', I had become a laissez-faire libertarian in the late 1960s. I became passionately committed to individual freedom and was deeply suspicious of state power. I began to believe that the state was 'a second-order phenomenon', at best a protector of what people choose to do in private. Now, I realise I was wrong. I now believe the state is of the first order. It can allow citizens to flourish or it can become a big obstacle to their realising their potential. To rise despite the state is courageous but it cannot become a long-term virtue. India should grow not at night but during the day.

Thus, I became a moderate classical liberal. I no longer

believed in a minimal, 'night watchman' state, and I wanted enlightened regulation of the market, state spending for public goods, especially education and health—although I didn't think the state ought to have a monopoly on running schools and hospitals—and a safety net for the poorest. I believe in a liberal democratic state that needs a vigorous civil society to make it accountable.

As a consequence of my conversion, I have realised that the Indian state should do a better job of governing rather than engage in the hundreds of things it has been asked to do. What India needs (even more than economic reforms) is to reform its governance. It should not take 12 years to get justice in the courts. One in four members in India's Parliament and state assemblies should not have a criminal record. The police should not be a handmaiden of the chief minister. A bureaucrat in the government should not be promoted on the basis of seniority but on performance and results. Only if it does this will India become a developed country one day.

~

A New Middle Class Attains Dignity

MILESTONE 24: INDIA, MAY 2014

If India won its political freedom in August 1947, and its economic freedom in July 1991, it attained middle-class dignity in May 2014. This is the significance of the landslide victory of a chai-walla's, a tea vendor's, son. Narendra Modi's success invites us to be imaginative in thinking about the nature of human dignity. A new middle class grew rapidly after the economic reforms—rising roughly from about ten per cent of the population to around a quarter—and gradually it began to change the country's rhetoric in favour of middle-class aspirations for a better life. By electing a chai-walla's son, the electorate affirmed the dreams of the millions who had pulled themselves up in the post-reform decades through their own efforts into the middle class. The elite class was forced to confront its Brahminical prejudice that selling groceries or driving a three-wheeler is socially beneath its dignity.

The typical voters who elected Modi in 2014 were not Hindu nationalists. They were young, middle-of-the-road people who had migrated from their villages to towns. They had got their first jobs and their first cell phones, and aspired to a life better than that of their parents.

Modi's relentless rhetoric of *vikas*, or development, during his election campaign gave them a sense of possibilities. (During his campaign, Modi mentioned *vikas* five hundred times for each time he uttered *Hindutva*, according to a computer analysis of his speeches by Dr Walter Andersen, a former US State Department official.) The chai-walla assuaged their other insecurities—they no longer needed to speak English in a certain way to get ahead. If the chai-walla could aspire to lead India without English, they too could be modern in their mother tongues. All they needed were the old-fashioned values of thrift, ambition and industry.

In her book *Bourgeois Dignity*, Deirdre McCloskey explains that the same thing happened during the 'great transformation' in the 19th-century West when the industrial revolution created a middle class that changed the master narrative of Western societies. John Ruskin, the 19th-century British art critic, once remarked that the greatest contribution that an aristocratic duke could make to the modern world would be to take a job as a grocer. This seemingly bizarre suggestion goes to the heart of middle-class dignity. Unequal, hierarchical societies need to correct their misguided notions about human worth and what constitutes a dignified life.

For young persons who had risen through their own initiative and hard work, *vikas* was a code word for opportunity in the competitive market, which Adam Smith called a 'natural system of liberty'. The government in this system was supposed to create an enabling environment that allowed free individuals to pursue their interests peacefully in an open, transparent market. After that, an 'invisible hand' would help to gradually lift people into a dignified, middle-class life. Underlying middle-class dignity is the economic freedom that the 1991 reforms brought to India as business decisions moved from the offices of politicians and bureaucrats to the marketplace.

Although the reforms have been slow, hesitant and incomplete, they have set in motion a process of profound change in Indian society. It is similar to the turning point of Deng's revolution in China in December 1978. Unlike China, however, India has practised democracy since Independence and it has been raising the lower castes through politics. Its affirmative action has taken the form of quotas for the historically oppressed castes in university seats and government jobs. Thus, the masses have gradually acquired a stake in the system, periodically electing representatives from the lowest castes. The reforms of 1991 accelerated this social process.

The other distinctive quality of India's modernity is that it embraced democracy before capitalism, which makes its path unique. In the rest of the world, democracy followed capitalism. This inversion means that India's future will not be a creation of unbridled forces of the market but will evolve through a dialogue between (1) the conservative forces of caste, religion and village; (2) the vocal forces of the left which continue to influence the country's intellectual life; and (3) the neoliberal forces of global capitalism. These negotiations of democracy mean that the pace of economic reforms is slow and incremental. It also explains why India is not growing as rapidly as the Asian tigers. The positive side is that its transition is more stable and negotiated than Russia's or China's, and is more likely to preserve its way of life and its diverse civilisation.

~

The Indian Liberal's Hopes Fade Over Time

MILESTONE 25: INDIA, 2014-2024

My hopes of Prime Minister Modi's government have faded over time. It began with the botched-up demonetisation of the currency in 2016. In an attempt to control 'black money' in the untaxed cash economy, the government suddenly withdrew Rs 500 and Rs 1000 notes. Instead of trapping rich tax evaders, the measure hurt small businesses and the poor in a country where 90 per cent of the transactions were in cash. If at all demonisation had to be done—and I am not sure about that—it would have been smarter to have quietly issued high-value currency notes (say Rs 5000 and Rs 10,000) and withdrawn only those after a few years when the black money had moved into the higher notes. Thus, ordinary lives would not have been disrupted as severely as they were. Then, the Modi government soon followed this up with the introduction of the Goods and Services Tax (GST), an excellent idea that unified the country, but again it was executed poorly, and it brought confusion and avoidable pain to small businesses.

The real cause of my unease, however, is the rise of militant Hindu nationalism, which has challenged India's cherished secular ideal of *sarva dharma samabhava*, respect for all religions. It has polarised the nation, creating an atmosphere of hate, making many Muslims feel insecure. While there has been no large-scale communal riot since 2014 (as in Gujarat in 2002 or in Delhi in 1984), there have occurred innumerable illiberal, intolerant acts. The victims of the localised violence usually were

Muslims suspected of selling beef. Since the perpetrators were supporters of the ruling party, the police acted like bystanders, and no action was taken against the guilty. The leadership of the party did not condemn the violence. Those who spoke up were condemned on social media as anti-national, and even arrested and denied bail.

The first incident was on 28 September 2015 in Bisahda, a village near Dadri in western Uttar Pradesh. Incited by an announcement from the temple's public address system, a mob gathered outside the home of a Muslim, Mohammed Akhlaq, and accused him of stealing a calf and slaughtering it for the upcoming Eid festival. They raided his fridge and found leftover meat curry, which was proof in their eyes that he had killed a cow. Akhlaq protested, saying that it was goat meat. Since no one believed him, he and his son were dragged out and beaten with rods and bricks. Akhlaq died from the assault; his son was seriously injured and had to undergo brain surgery. The police arrested eight persons but the accused were soon out on bail. The BJP tried to distance itself from this incident. A minister, Mahesh Sharma, claimed it was an 'accident'. Prime Minister Modi spoke out but only after ten days.

The Akhlaq lynching set a pattern. In the name of

gau raksha, 'cow protection', vigilantes began to assault Muslims, accusing them of killing cows or transporting them for slaughter. In March 2016, two cattle traders were lynched in Jharkhand and their bodies hung from a tree. In July 2016, four Dalits were assaulted in Una, Gujarat for skinning dead cows. In 2017, a dairy farmer, Pehlu Khan, was attacked on a busy highway in Rajasthan and his lynching was filmed and posted on social media. The six men accused by Khan in his dying declaration were let go by the police. In June 2018, another lynching in Hapur, Uttar Pradesh was filmed on mobile phones. There are no official statistics of hate crimes in India but some media houses have offered varying estimates. *IndiaSpend* reported 118 attacks. *Quint* claimed that 88 persons died between 2015 and 2018. A resurgence in gau raksha vigilance resulted in a slump in the cattle economy in the states of Uttar Pradesh, Rajasthan, Gujarat and Madhya Pradesh. Farmers who would earlier sell their barren cows and unproductive bulls found no buyers. Feral cattle were left to roam and they rampaged the fields, looking for sustenance, thereby ruining standing crops.

Another significant threat to religious freedom came with the passage of the Citizenship Amendment Act, 2019 (CAA). It aimed to provide a path to citizenship for minorities from neighbouring countries, but it excluded Muslims. People feared that this law, together with the proposed National Register of Citizens (NRC), would create a religious test for citizenship and would end in disenfranchising Muslims. CAA led to massive protests across the country, and these were put down with a heavy hand by the police detaining hundreds of people.

I was particularly distressed at the way the Foreign Contributions (Regulation) Act (FCRA) was misused to shut down inconvenient civil society and non-government organisations (NGOs). In 2023, the FCRA licence of the much-admired think tank, Centre for Policy Research (CPR) was cancelled. It meant that the think tank could no longer raise international funding. No one could explain why this happened, for CPR is a centrist think tank, not a vocal critic of the government. Amnesty International and Oxfam India had suffered the same fate, as did 20,693 other NGOs. Originally, the FCRA was meant to prevent overseas funding of elections. But it now turned into a weapon to shut down critics of the government. In closing the door to international philanthropy, the many excellent programmes to lift the poor have been closed. In the case of think tanks like CPR, academic excellence, independent research and the freedom to think have lost out.

There has been steady erosion of liberal democracy in India. If democracy was only about free and fair elections, India would be counted as an undoubted success. For a messy, third-world country, it clearly has free and fair elections. However, a healthy democracy goes beyond elections to robust institutions, such as the judiciary, the press, the police, the Central Bureau of Investigation, the Central Vigilance Commission, the Election Commission, the Enforcement Directorate, etc. During the 2014 campaign, I had assumed our institutions were reasonably independent and robust and could be depended on to keep civil liberties safe. This has turned out to be untrue. We have seen the slow capture of these institutions. A small but telling example was the sad sight of the retired Chief Justice of India (CJI), Ranjan Gogoi being rewarded with an appointment to the Rajya Sabha, undermining, in my eyes, judicial independence.

To be fair, I must also mention that Narendra Modi's government has done a number of positive things. It ushered in a digital revolution that almost doubled the banking population and is formalising the economy. It managed to enact a much-needed bankruptcy law, so crucial to a market economy. It has been far more efficient than its predecessors in delivering welfare benefits to the poor, such as cooking gas and toilets in rural homes. These explain Modi's continuing popularity at the polls. But it is also true that his government has failed to enact important structural reforms—land acquisition, labour codes and farm laws—partly because of opposition in the parliament. Most importantly, the Modi government has done no better than its predecessors to create an industrial revolution and deliver the promised jobs.

~

How to Live in the World

MILESTONE 26: MADRAS MUSEUM, EGMORE, CHENNAI, SEPTEMBER 2015

A day in September, 2015. I have a few hours to kill before my flight in Madras and I decide to visit a museum in Egmore. While I am admiring a Chola bronze from the 11th century, created in the once great city of Tanjore, a middle-aged, barefoot woman in a six-foot South Indian saree is standing behind me. I make way for her. Without self-consciousness, she comes forward and puts a vermilion mark on the Shiva Nataraja. I am appalled. Doesn't she realise this is a museum, not a temple?

I soon realise that we live in different worlds. Mine is secular; hers is sacred. Both of us stand before the bronze statue with different expectations. For me, it is a 900-year-old object of beauty; for her, it is God. Mine is aesthetic pleasure; hers is divine *darshana*. She doesn't see what I see, a brilliant work in bronze by an early Chola artist. I admire the weightless joy of the dancer, so skilfully captured by the sculptor. I move along, passing by other bronzes, getting irritated when the bronzes are dusty, or ill lit, or poorly spaced. But just as quickly, I feel embarrassed about my petty concerns, my niggling mind.

I look for the woman after a while. She is still there, absorbed by her light-footed, tireless prancing god, whose dance actually brings the universe into being. Without missing a beat, and in the fullness of time, he dances it out of existence. There is a luxuriant richness in her sacred world, compared to the poverty of my weary, feeble and secular existence. To her, the beat of the drum in Shiva's right hand announces a momentous event. The flame in his left hand is telling her that the universe is about to be created. His lower right hand bestows upon her freedom from fear. His raised left arm is a symbol of her release. For someone carrying out such a momentous mission, her god looks cool, athletic and debonair.

My modern, secular, English-speaking life, in comparison, seems empty. I will never know the depth, the opulence of her world. My secular friends will be quick to brand her superstitious, illiterate and casteist. But she is probably more tolerant, accepting of diversity, because she is capable of seeing God everywhere. She thus has something to teach both the secularists of the Congress Party and the Hindu nationalists of the BJP. They might even learn the real meaning of secularism from her—that the practice of religion is a very private pursuit, to be respected and left to the individual.

In my world of museums, concert halls, and bookstores, there is plenty of search for beauty but no place for the holy. When Nietzsche taught that 'God is dead,' he meant that modern, secular individuals like me had lost the possibility of faith. The meaninglessness of a non-believer's life has brought us to an absurd situation. Sartre and Camus had offered consolation—'Man creates his own meaning,' they said—but that is easier said than done. The life of my fellow museum visitor, on the other hand, held the possibility of fullness and wholeness of being.

I turn to look once again at the statue of Shiva Nataraja. He is still unperturbed, absorbed in the serious business of creating and destroying the universe. There is something new, however. Under his raised left leg is a marigold flower! I decide that the next time the world gets too much for me, I shall go and visit a museum. If I'm not careful, I too might experience eternity.

This is a true story and my favourite. It revealed to me that I had matured as a liberal and learned how to respond to someone of the opposite belief to mine with openness, respect and an ability to appreciate with quiet patience the very best qualities in the other person's belief. I recommend it as an ethically responsible way to live in the world.

~

The Decline of Liberal Democracy in the World

MILESTONE 27: 2015-2024

In the third decade of the 21st century, when I am writing this book, liberal democracy is threatened across the world, as many governments are being captured by demagogues. These charismatic, often amoral populists have all been elected to power by a large majority of their people. It is almost a rejection of democracy as we have known it.

There are a number of reasons for the diminishing faith in liberal democracy. There have been losers in a globalisation based on free trade and open borders. Living standards of ordinary people in the West have been stagnating for decades. The liberal ideal of an equal, multi-ethnic society has resulted in a backlash against immigration, exacerbated by racial and religious prejudice. Average citizens feel that public bureaucracies are callous and self-serving, and do not respond to their needs. Nor do legislators reflect popular opinion because of their elite backgrounds and, increasingly, staggering money power. The popular anger is especially directed at the elites who have ruled and benefitted the most from the post-1945 international liberal order. They run the public and private sectors and are hopelessly out of touch. To top it all, social media has amplified the discontent, especially the radical voices of extremists.

Amid the prevailing pessimism of the ordinary person, populists have entered the fray, convincing people that they alone reflect the 'people's will'. They place majoritarian issues, such as immigration and unwelcome minorities, on the policy agenda. Once in power, they begin to slowly subvert the independent, liberal institutions of democracy, repress the press and the opposition. They stop respecting constitutional rights and soon become brazenly illiberal. Gradually the rule of law begins to erode. Then, checks and balances disappear, and eventually free and fair elections cease. In the end, these countries become electoral dictatorships. Countries ranging from Venezuela to Hungary to Turkey illustrate this pattern.

The lesson is that a liberal democracy has two parts: democracy *and* liberalism. When populists come to power, they first undermine the independence of governance institutions such as the police and the judiciary. This undercuts the rule of law and often violates the rights of minorities. Illiberal democracy is a distinct regime in its own right, as Fareed Zakaria pointed out more than two decades ago in an essay, 'The Rise of Illiberal Democracy'. He cited evidence from Yugoslavia, Philippines, Peru, Pakistan and more. The worrisome fact is that since then the world's two largest democracies, United States and India, have also weakened. The strength of American democracy used to lie in its vocal civic associations—as Tocqueville pointed out in his classic, *Democracy in America*—which mediated between the citizen and the state and, together, were a bulwark against illiberal behaviour. But these institutions have eroded. India does not possess such civic associations. The associational life of most Indians is traditional, caste based. Moreover, India's nascent governance institutions are also weaker. In the long run, it may be harder to repair any damage to the liberal order.

~

Is the Curtain Closing on a Liberal Age?

MILESTONE 28: JANUARY 2024

As I near the end of my life, I wonder if the curtain is closing on the liberal age. Over two centuries, liberal democracy grew around the world, making it, on the whole, more prosperous, stable and humane than perhaps it had ever been before. My own life too was defined by the second liberal order which began after the Second World War. The past 75 years have been surprisingly successful for the liberal creed: not only have we been spared world wars, we have also witnessed the spread of democracy, open markets, globalisation and generous welfare states. This international liberal age is now under threat as the world is relapsing into illiberal nationalism, autocracy and fundamentalism.

History did not end in 1989. Thirty years after the fall of the Berlin Wall, new narrow nationalisms and populisms have emerged. Liberal norms and institutions are eroding in many democracies. Eastern Europe is relapsing. The Islamic model has failed in the Middle East. Assertive authoritarian leaders, like Xi Jinping in China and Vladimir Putin in Russia, have risen. Brexit in the UK and Donald Trump in America are symbols of anti-immigration movements. India, a beacon of liberalism in the East, is threatened by the rise of authoritarian Hindu nationalism. People's rhetoric is hopelessly polarised.

Narrow nationalism around the world is leading to protectionist tariff walls being erected in many countries. This will make it more difficult for a country like India to export in the future. Although India has grown at almost 7% a year for 30 years—an enviable achievement for a democracy—it has still not created enough jobs to take away surplus farm labour into more productive, higher-income pursuits. India has, in short, not created an 'industrial revolution'. All successful nations in recent times have done this in the same manner after Japan showed the way in the decades following the Second World War. It was through the export of simple, labour-intensive manufactured goods. China's success is the latest example of this model. With rising protectionism in world trade, India's aspirations will be more difficult to achieve.

Liberalism has frankly turned out to be more fragile than we imagined. Some believe the cause of the problem is rising inequality. Globalisation has produced winners and losers, and the losers are revolting against the elites who created this system. Others blame liberalism for failing to appreciate the value of identity and community in human life. The demand for dignity and respect explains movements such as Black Lives Matter, #MeToo, and much of campus politics. The fact is that liberalism depends on the rational side of human nature, but the desire for identity and dignity appeals to our emotional side. Classical liberalism would be happier if human differences didn't matter. It is thus a struggle between two legitimate human ends.

The consolation in my old age is that history has proven to be cyclical. The identities that people embrace today are the identities their children will want to escape from tomorrow. So, it is a matter of time—hopefully—before the rational side of human nature will assert itself again. There are plenty of other reasons to be hopeful about liberalism's future, and I shall come back to them at the end of the book.

6

Liberalism's Shortcomings

In which I confess that I am uncomfortable with certain deficiencies in the liberal creed and its practice. But the solutions are equally unsatisfactory.

My unease with liberalism begins with the overwhelming stress on the individual, and it ends with some of the weaknesses in democracy and capitalism themselves. While I admire the liberal ideal of the intrinsic worth of an individual, I find it does not value enough the bonds of community. The smooth running of society is based on an interdependence of individuals in which they respect each other's freedom. By ignoring social life, liberals overlook the alienated, lonely, disconnected existence of individuals in large, modern cities and towns. Excessive emphasis on personal success and competition at the workplace is one of the causes of the problem.

Liberals need to remember Aristotle's maxim that a human being is a political and social animal. They need to restore in their thinking 'fraternity', the third part of the French Revolution's cry, and one of the central principles of the Indian Constitution. Along with liberty and equality, liberals must learn to value the collective life. Human beings are not isolated and disconnected—at least not by choice. They engage daily with children, parents, relatives, friends and colleagues. They express themselves as free, equal moral persons within the many associations of their communities. The rise in nationalism in the world today may well be a subconscious craving for community, especially by citizens who have lost out in globalisation.

The notion of the self-interested individual is a useful starting point in classical liberal economics, and it has influenced profoundly the development of other social sciences and of utilitarian philosophy. While self-interest is important to human survival, it tends to run the risk of excess, crossing the line into selfishness. When it rains, I carry an umbrella—nothing selfish about that. But when I am willing to step on another's toes to get what I want, my self-interest becomes negative. There are other problems with excessive egoistic desire—self-importance, vanity, expecting continuous premium treatment. On the other hand, liberal theory has ignored the fact that human beings are not always self-interested, they sometimes tend to behave selflessly. My discomfort with liberalism is that it undervalues other moral sentiments such as altruism and compassion, thus misrepresenting reality.

These failings of liberalism are not new. They were first voiced in the 19th century by romantics, socialists and utopians. These critics were reacting against Enlightenment's rationalism and the negative consequences of industrial capitalism. They questioned not only the individualist premises of liberalism, but also expressed concern about the vast impersonal forces of modern institutions unleashed by the industrial revolution. They felt that unrestricted freedom of liberalism would lead to anarchy and the dissolution of society. They lamented the decline in the collective life of the village.

The most virulent critic of liberalism was Karl Marx, who believed that capitalism's individualism was based on callous self-interest which led to the heartless laws of the market. Capitalist bourgeois society, he felt, had broken the bonds of community. The worker had got alienated from his work and had become dehumanised like a cog in the industrial machine. Marx's solution was to restore humanity to the worker via common ownership of the means of production. He called it socialism, and this would lead to an egalitarian utopia called communism. His idea was experimented with in the 20th century, first in Soviet Russia, then in Eastern Europe, Mao's China and North Korea—everywhere with tragic consequences. His egalitarian assumption turned out to be too idealistic because, as I have noted before, the human ego will not shrink that far. It needs incentives for performance. To retain ideological purity, communism also needs autocratic rule, which eventually snatches away the individual's freedom, as happened in the Soviet Union and Eastern Europe, and continues to happen in China and North Korea.

Mahatma Gandhi in India had similar problems with liberalism. Although he was profoundly liberal by temperament, he was equally critical of modern European civilisation based on Enlightenment's rationality and industrial capitalism. The Industrial Revolution had introduced machine-based production that made possible an endless supply of commodities. These increased human desires, making people want more. Wanting more led to competition and conflict. Violence was thus embedded in the market economy. Hence, Gandhi rejected industrialisation, urban life and modern civilisation. He believed that genuine civilisation was to be found in the self-governing, self-sufficient villages of India where traditional life was governed by a common morality where each person performed his duty. It was the opposite of modern society, which operated on the basis of self-interest and individual goals. Gandhi's utopia was based on individuals operating through a chain of reciprocity linked to each other through a sense of dharma, moral duty. It too was equally idealistic—and perhaps harmful too, as in his uncritical faith in the Indian village, which Ambedkar called a 'den of narrow-mindedness' and inequality. Many of Gandhi's colleagues realised this during India's freedom movement, and his utopian idea was never put into practice.

There were other communitarian critiques of liberalism but none questioned the absolute value of freedom or liberty. On the contrary, most of them argued that by reducing everything to the level of the individual, liberalism was in practice diminishing and impoverishing the idea of liberty. Freedom, like human life itself, was being divided, becoming fragmentary and emasculated. Such critiques of liberalism attempted to bring back to human lives a wholeness, a sense of unity expressed under the old French Revolution banner of 'Liberty, Equality and Fraternity'. Indeed, the debate of 'community versus the individual' became the most celebrated among early sociologists—Tönnies, Durkheim, Simmel, Weber—prompted by the breakdown of the traditional bonds of society by industrialisation. Even today, the continuing popularity of democratic socialism on the left reflects a preference for social solidarity as opposed to individualism. On the right, nationalism shows a preference for social solidarity through national identity.

During my early years in America, I was much influenced by the French traveller Alexis de Tocqueville's views about American life. In his classic *Democracy in America*, he observed that Americans were in the habit of joining voluntary groups in their local communities—baseball leagues, parent-teacher associations, girl scouts, bridge groups, book clubs, etc. I too had observed this. I found that when neighbours met, they naturally discussed issues concerning their neighbourhood, such as the quality of the local school, trash collection, lights on the street, and so on. This engagement at the local level, Tocqueville believed, embedded democratic 'habits of the heart', making democracy work at the national level.

Many years later, I met the political scientist Robert Putnam at Harvard and read his book *Bowling Alone*. It introduced me to the concept of 'social capital' and helped me to better understand Tocqueville's idea of how 'joining' at the local level helps build trust in society. It makes possible the individual free choice of liberalism, and leads to a cohesive society. Putnam was rightly worried that the advent of television, the automobile, suburbia and the Internet were eroding the rich community life of earlier America. He felt this decline in social capital was eroding American democracy. I shall return to this theme when I discuss the rise of illiberal democracy in the world.

As a liberal, I have finally understood that social capital provides an underlying glue that leads people to trust each other in the market and the state. It, in fact, makes capitalism and democracy possible. Repeated interactions between people builds trust between individuals. In the marketplace, it reduces transaction costs of economic exchange, and reduces the need for legal contracts or government oversight and regulation. Having social capital, Francis Fukuyama points out, is a major reason why America was able to build large, impersonal corporations, unlike many other nations.

In recent years, liberalism has come under criticism

from contemporary communitarians as well. The Israeli-American sociologist Amitai Etzioni argues that a community rather than individuals should formulate basic human values such as the concept of the good. His ideas have influenced politicians of the Third Way like Bill Clinton in the United States and Tony Blair in Britain. 'Social capital' became a buzz word among these politicians because they were able to attract floating voters with a promise of lower taxes and limited government; these voters had been put off earlier by the crass neoliberal arrogance of Margaret Thatcher and Ronald Reagan. The buzz words of community, voluntarism, civic virtue and neighbourly responsibility were like gifts to explain to voters poverty, street crime and urban anomie as the results of erosion of community.

While social capital is a sound idea, my problem with contemporary communitarians is that too often they want the state to enforce a form of moral paternalism in order to achieve the goal of a rich community life. They want to impose a particular behaviour on a free people and force them to speak and act in a certain way. While their diagnosis of the decline in social capital is correct, I find extending state power into people's private lives profoundly illiberal.

I'm also not impressed with some other ideas of contemporary communitarians. Richard Layard, a Labour economist and MP, believes that working too hard is a source of unhappiness in capitalist economies; hence, work should be taxed more heavily, so that people will substitute leisure for work. The French did, in fact, put this in practice by legislating a 35-hour week, but I am not sure if happiness improved in France. My French friends tell me that it reduced output and made the country less competitive. Another bizarre idea is that of John Roemer, a leftist economist, who believes that most inequalities in the modern economy are due to differing intelligence or IQ of people; hence, intellectual endowments of individuals should be taxed more heavily. New Labour in the UK did actually implement this idea, although in a softer form. It made university education a right in order to end social exclusion—there was no merit criterion at entry. It went further; it wanted universities to stop grades or marks, so that everyone would have an equal chance in the labour market.

Yet, although I am an enthusiastic liberal, I too have found obvious deficiencies in the liberal creed and its practice. The excessive emphasis on individualism does weaken a sense of community. The solutions proposed, however, for civic engagement and a just collective life are unsatisfactory. Various attempts to create a just community have too often taken away the individual's freedom. I have still not been able to resolve the contradiction between the excellent European Enlightenment ideals from which many anti-colonial movements drew inspiration, and the practice of colonialism by European colonisers, who denied those ideals to the people they ruled. It is true that early liberals suffered from racism, but that does not make liberalism a creed of imperialism or racism or white supremacy, as critics like Conor Cruise O'Brien, Uday Mehta, Pankaj Mishra and others have implied.

I am also discouraged by the failings of capitalism. Its tendency to inequality is at the heart of the problem which keeps wealth and power with a few. The corporation is also under attack today. 'Obscene' CEO salaries are an example. Ever since Gladstone's 1862 Companies Act created the modern corporation, there have been attempts to reform it. One idea is to adopt the stakeholder capitalism of Germany and Japan to replace the shareholder capitalism of the Anglo-American classical liberal tradition. The stakeholder model is more accountable to employees, suppliers, debtors and the community, and not just to shareholders. Although more ethical, it has not been adopted more broadly because the shareholder model has performed far better in innovation and efficiency. However, the regulation of corporate governance has tightened in many countries in recent years, including in India. But capitalism needs to do more in order to restore trust in society.

There is indeed a crisis of liberalism today. The left complains about rampant commercialism and inequality; the right complains about narcissistic elites, atomisation in society and loss in traditional values. Some of liberalism's problems are its own fault. Excessive individualism, as I have noted, erodes a sense of community. Lonely, alienated individuals become prey to nationalist appeals of populist leaders against immigrants and minorities. Certainly, capitalism and democracy need correcting everywhere. Both need reform from time to time. But the critics of liberalism are unhelpful, unable to offer better alternatives. Many people equate liberalism with American hegemony. America's failings in Vietnam and Iraq were not moral failures of liberalism but failings of geopolitical power. Would the world be a better place if the liberal norms of the international order were to be scrapped? When it comes to geopolitics, would Indians be happier if America withdrew from Asia, allowing China to dominate it completely? There is always a need for more justice and equality in the world, but it seems to me that the historic gains from liberalism have been hugely positive over the past two centuries. As of now, there is no viable alternative to the liberal way.

7

The Dilemma of an Indian Liberal

In which I narrate some of the dilemmas, ironies and paradoxes I have encountered. In this journey. I have discovered, sadly, that the liberal is on a lonely road.

The dilemma of the Indian liberal begins at home. One morning, my leftish son drops in for a cup of coffee. He asks insistently, 'Dad, how can you be so calm about Hindu nationalism. You are a dithering liberal, treating both sides as if they are equal. Meanwhile, the right is spewing such hateful talk on social media. Shouldn't you call out evil when you see it?'

I tell him that our Constitution guarantees us freedom

of speech, allowing people to say both the things we approve of and the things we don't. I remind him about Voltaire's famous line: 'I do not agree with a word you say but I will defend to the death your right to say it.'

'I don't know anyone who will defend to the death what he believes in,' he sighs in resignation.

Later in the morning, I think some more about our conversation and I feel embarrassed. My son does have a point. It is important to speak up in a liberal democracy. I remember how upset I was in 2011 seeing honest Prime Minister Manmohan Singh presiding silently over a corrupt government. I admired him as a soft-spoken reformer and I felt let down. I wrote a column in the *Times of India* titled, 'Don't be Silent, Prime Minister!' It was triggered by the telecom spectrum scandal of his corrupt minister. The PM, it turned out, had known what his minister was up to. He had, in fact, advised him against it. But the minister had gone ahead anyway. Five years later, I was equally upset when Prime Minister Modi remained silent at the atrocities against Muslims, and again I raised the question in another column in the *Times of India.*

A few days later, my mind broadens to the national canvas and to another paradox. The fact is that democracy is not natural. It is built on inherent contradictions and needs constant vigilance, cultivation and education. Our Constitution makers realised this and tried to reconcile two contrary ends by laying down a system of checks and balances, mainly through separation of powers between the legislature (Parliament), executive (primarily, the prime minister and cabinet) and the judiciary. On the one hand, majority rule is a rational ideal and it has to prevail; on the other hand, once a majority gains power, it will not only work for the common good but will also work for its own advantage and try to fulfil its own agenda. Democracy's success lies in how it manages to balance this tension. Thus, in addition to respect for the checks-and-balances system prescribed by the Constitution, it is the job of political leaders to keep citizens well informed; instil in them democratic habits of the heart; and teach them liberal etiquette so that they behave with equality and mutual respect. But all around us, in India and the world, political leaders are turning away from this responsibility. In fact, many of them are doing exactly the opposite.

Returning to my son's question, I wonder how a liberal deals with rising illiberalism. How to manage in today's polarised environment? In India, liberal Muslims and liberal Hindus face different challenges, which they try to address in distinctive ways. The recent rise of identity politics, majoritarianism and nationalism adds to the urgency. How does a liberal uphold the universal principles of secularism in a country of such religious diversity without disrespecting the rights, traditions and personal laws of different religious communities?

There are other dilemmas. At a time when India is rising economically and poised to become a major global player as a democratic counterweight to a dictatorial China, its independent democratic institutions are weakening. Critics are being silenced, the discourse in social media is turning not only right-wing but hateful. How to deal with a conflict between the liberal value of free speech and maintaining harmony in society? Liberals are torn: should they support the freedom of expression or oppose hate speech that hurts a community and incites violence?

How to harmonise the demands of inclusivity and social justice with the liberal creed of equal treatment? Growing demands for reservations are narrowing the scope for a meritocratic society. How does a liberal deal with the politics of identity and reservations? To achieve the cherished value of social justice, a liberal must find ways to address the concerns of individuals caught between their duty to caste, language and religion.

Then there is the irony relating to democracy versus

prosperity. India was once admired and envied as a vigorous democracy but it was a poorly performing economy. Now it has a dynamic, rapidly growing economy but democracy is weakening. India won its freedom in 1947 but it promptly lost its economic freedom to a socialist command economy for the next four decades. It finally won economic freedom in 1991 and soon went on to become the second-fastest-growing economy in the world. It had achieved the liberal dream. But just when everything seemed to be going well, democracy began to decline in the second decade of the 21st century. Why must economic freedom come at the cost of political freedom or social harmony?

How to balance the freedom of the market with the need for a social safety net for the poorest and the most disadvantaged in a country with limited resources? How to ameliorate the tendency of the market towards inequality? How to cope with the demands of economic growth and the imperative of conserving the environment? Why is it important to 'sell' market reforms to the public?

These are the sorts of the issues faced by Indian liberals. I shall discuss some of them below, and in this order: (1) How does a liberal cope in a polarised environment? (2) Who does a liberal vote for when none of the alternatives is suitable? (3) What is the hope for a liberal party in

India? (3) Since a liberal is unelectable, he or she tends to join a mainstream party, hoping to make a difference from within. How then to navigate inside a coalition that advocates illiberal causes? (4) How does one deal with nationalism that is ascendant worldwide? (5) The 'Liberal Fallacy' is about the difficulty of doing liberal reforms in a poor democracy. Is this true? (6) What are the distinctive challenges of liberal Hindus and liberal Muslims? (7) How does a young, sexually liberated person respond to prudish, conservative parents? (8) Can political and economic freedom go together? And finally (9), with the rise of illiberal democracies, where do we go from here?

Living in a polarised environment

When I switched in the 1960s from Nehruvian socialism to classical liberalism and joined the Swatantra Party, my friends thought me odd, but they did not shun me. Everyone was a socialist then. They were disappointed that I had abandoned my principles and sold out to capitalism. Yet, I did not lose a single friend. No one rejected me for my politics. This is no longer true today. The political environment is depressingly polarised these days—you are either a friend or a foe. You either love Modi or hate him.

The same thing happened when I was in college in

America. My professors and fellow students were liberals. Liberalism was the reigning ideology of the age. Yet they did not reject their conservative colleagues just because they were conservatives. The latter could rant all they wanted against Roosevelt's New Deal or bluster in favour of greater American aggression in the Cold War. The liberals would argue back, but they would not shut them down. Today, it is no longer easy to be a conservative at an American university; nor is it prudent to argue too loudly against Trump in the conservative heartlands.

When agricultural reforms were announced in 2021 by the Modi government, repealing three existing highly statist farm laws, I was delighted and wrote a column predicting a second green revolution. Many of my sensible friends, however, criticised the move just because they disliked Modi. Of course, the government too did wrong in trying to push the reforms hastily through the Parliament without a debate. It did not engage with the protesters until it was too late. Every reformer needs to remember Margaret Thatcher's advice that she spent 20 per cent of her time reforming and 80 per cent selling the reforms. There is never a good alternative to dialogue and transparency.

I felt the three proposed farm bills offered three freedoms to farmers. One, they could now sell anywhere to anyone, freeing them from the shackles of a monopoly cartel at the state-controlled mandi. Second, both farmers and traders got the freedom to store inventory which had been constrained by stocking limits in the Essential Commodities Act. It gave the incentive for cold storages to come up, to whom farmers could now sell directly. Third, it gave farmers the freedom to make forward contracts, transferring their risk to businessmen.

Who could be against farmers, the majority of Indians, finally winning economic freedom—the kind that Indian industry had won 30 years ago and the Chinese farmer 40 years ago? Although the opposition to the farm bills came mainly from a few states of the north-west, it was generously financed by vested trading interests. Seeing this as an opportunity to embarrass an increasingly authoritarian government, the opposition parties and intellectuals also rose against the reform. Sadly, the liberal reforms were withdrawn and the opportunity for a second green revolution was lost.

Living through those sad months was disheartening. Even more depressing was the realisation that illiberal statism is still India's reigning ideology 30 years after the 1991 reforms. The Hindu nationalist wants a strong, macho state, and national security is at the top of its agenda. This has led to irrational curbs on Chinese imports, for example, which have hurt India far more than China. Leftists have always been statist, ready to expand the public sector and enhance government controls on the economy. The caste-parties in the states believe in a *mai-baap sarkar* which can solve their problems through enhancing quotas for their castes. All across the political spectrum, there is a preference for an often restrictive, oppressive social solidarity as opposed to empowering individualism. The conception of an independent, rights-bearing individual loses out in favour of a person's membership in a community. Both the left and the right take the state to be the new locus of that community—in contrast to the liberal conception of the state as a neutral arbiter of private rights.

Who shall I vote for?

My fear at election time is always the same—that one of the two main candidates will win. In 2014, India was a discontented, politically troubled nation. People were sick of the drift and paralysis in the government. It was similar in some ways to Britain in the late 1970s. Britain yearned then for a strong leader and it got Margaret Thatcher. In India, we got Narendra Modi. The election took place in May that year. Sickened by the corruption and deadness of the Congress-led UPA coalition, I was clutching at straws.

I didn't feel enthusiastic about any of the alternatives. A start-up, Aam Aadmi Party, had risen out of the ashes of Anna Hazare's anti-corruption movement, but it wasn't yet a serious contender. The other parties were regional. I yearned for the long dead Swatantra Party, the only true liberal party India has ever had. In this unhappy state, the only serious alternative seemed to be the right-wing BJP. It was led by Narendra Modi, whose sudden rise to power in the BJP had caught everyone by surprise. I was nervous because he was supposed to be authoritarian and polarising and carried the stain of Hindu-Muslim riots in Gujarat in 2002.

I was worried at the time that India had a narrow window of opportunity which came from being a uniquely young nation. If those in the working age could find jobs, the gains in overall prosperity would far outweigh the burden of supporting the old and the very young. Economists call this a 'demographic dividend' which has historically provided a kick-start to GDP growth. If we elected the right candidate, prosperity would enter into millions of lives, and in course of time India would become a middle-class country. This window would close in a dozen years or so as India also began to age. Among the candidates in the 2014 elections, Modi seemed to be the best hope to deliver on the demographic dividend.

Modi's campaign speeches were surprisingly fresh. With a single-minded focus on *vikas*—a code word for investment, jobs, skills and growth—he sounded like a reformer. His slogan of 'minimum government, maximum governance' was music to my liberal ears. There is always a trade-off at the ballot box. The question in my mind was: 'Should I risk secularism and pluralism for the sake of prosperity, jobs and clean government?' I agonised for weeks. I reasoned that there had been no further Hindu-Muslim riots in Gujarat for more than a decade—perhaps he had turned a new leaf. It was a conflict in my mind between economic and religious freedom.

I was aware of the risks—Modi, as I have noted, was widely believed to be polarising, sectarian and authoritarian—but I felt the risk in not voting for him was greater. If India failed to create enough jobs, it would sacrifice another generation. Besides, India's democratic institutions were strong enough to prevent a dictatorial or communalised state. I did not absolve Modi of the stain of 2002, but I argued that job creation was as great a moral imperative as secularism. The alternative to Modi was Rahul Gandhi—a 'princeling' of the Nehru-Gandhi dynasty that had ruled India for most of the past 65 years—and he did not even come close.

In the end, I decided to vote for the BJP. I felt I had taken a calculated risk, and millions of Indians agreed with me. Modi swept the polls. I was among the first liberals to publicly endorse him in my column in the *Times of India*. My friends on the left thought I was either blind to what they saw as evil, or swept naively by the Modi wave. Those on the right did not accept me either—they were rightly suspicious because I had stridently rebuked Mr Modi for the 2002 riots in my columns.

The resentment that brought Narendra Modi to power in India in 2014 is similar to what elevated Donald Trump in the United States. Its roots lay in feelings of humiliation, envy and powerlessness. In India, the ordinary person felt excluded from the world of the English-educated elite which stepped into the shoes of the departing White sahibs at Independence; the elite had since monopolised power, wealth and privilege for almost 70 years. Since the serious business of the world continued to be transacted in an incomprehensible language, the vast majority of Indians felt condemned to be deaf and dumb in their own land. The same liberal ruling class adopted the excellent idea of secularism. But it did not bother to have a dialogue with the dharmic tradition that was part of the daily lives of the masses, as Mahatma Gandhi had done during the freedom struggle. In fact, the left elite looked down on the ritualistic polytheism of the intensely religious majority, making it feel degraded and insecure. Neither did the new rulers reform colonial institutions, nor fashion a new modernity, truer to the spirit of a free nation. These are some of the reasons that led to the rise of an assertive, strident Hindu nationalism.

By electing a chai-walla's son in 2014, the voter also affirmed the aspirations of the millions who had pulled themselves up through their own efforts into the middle class in the post-reform decades. The hopes, dreams, and dignity of an aspiring middle class were affirmed for the first time. Modi's rise had given them dignity—especially to people such as the kirana-walla, the autodriver, the carpenter, etc. He made millions believe that their future was open and could be altered by their own actions. You did not have to be upper class or speak English in a certain way to get ahead. If the chai-walla could aspire to lead India without a public-school English-language education, they too could be modern in their mother tongue. The same thing, as we have observed earlier, had happened during the 'great transformation' in the West when the industrial revolution created a middle class and gave it dignity, changing thus the master narrative of Western societies.

Reckoning in 2024

India, a country of 1.4 billion, goes to the polls in the spring of 2024 in the world's largest electoral exercise, in which 900 million citizens are registered to vote. Although my hopes of him have faded over time, Narendra Modi remains hugely popular after ten years in office. It is not only because of Hindu nationalism but because his government has done a far better job in delivering welfare benefits. Most rural families have access to urban amenities like toilets, cooking gas, electricity and drinking water. Governance has improved through Digital Public Infrastructure (DPI). Comprising a triad of identity, payments and data management, DPI has empowered citizens who previously lacked access to banking, health insurance and other areas, while reducing the scope for corruption by bypassing intermediaries and facilitation payments. Thus, the average citizen's interface with the state has improved. The economy too has performed reasonably well, although it has not created the desired number of jobs. Infrastructure has improved significantly. Democracy has weakened with the erosion of a free and independent press, but elections remain relatively free and fair both at the state and national level.

Yet, as a liberal, I find it difficult to vote for the

majoritarian, identity politics of the BJP as it is today. Muslims feel insecure, and with good reason. Democracy may be robust at the electoral level but its institutions and its liberal system of checks and balances have been undermined. Press freedom and free speech have been compromised and there is creeping authoritarianism. India is rightly called an illiberal democracy today. It is ironical that this has happened at the very moment when the country's global stature has risen, and India is increasingly seen in the world as a democratic counterweight to China.

If I cannot vote for the illiberal politics of the BJP, I do not trust the opposition either. In the past ten years, the opposition parties have not come up with a new idea to solve India's real problems such as jobs, education, healthcare and air quality. Handing out free electricity, pocket money to women or free bus rides will not cut it. The DNA of the Congress Party is redistributive and statist, ever ready to make a false trade-off between growth and equity. To be fair, some of the earlier ideas of the Congress, such as food security and the rural jobs guarantee did come to the rescue of the Modi government during the Covid crisis. But the Congress has no big ideas, no clear vision for economic progress, or even social empowerment. India desperately needs a viable opposition, and I was pleased to see the establishment of a grand coalition—the Indian National Developmental Inclusive Alliance (I.N.D.I.A) of more than two dozen political parties. But I have concerns about its viability. It has too many tired generals with big egos and small armies. It seems a difficult task for the Congress Party to unite harmoniously its many regional partners behind a positive vision to create an effective alliance. Even if it succeeds—which appears unlikely, as some allies are already parting ways with it—I do not see it as having the capability to execute vigorously the economic and governance reforms that the nation needs.

Rahul Gandhi of the Congress Party rightly warns the nation of the dangers of dictatorship. But his warnings are undermined by his own party's illiberal sins. It was his grandmother, Indira Gandhi, who began the rot in the 1970s, fashioning personalised governance, eroding collective decision-making, suppressing dissent and filling the jails with political opponents. After the Emergency, his well-meaning father, Rajiv Gandhi, compromised liberal values of gender justice, free speech and secularism by nullifying the Supreme Court's decision in the Shah Bano case—thus denying a Muslim woman maintenance after divorce from her husband—and banning Salman Rushdie's *The Satanic Verses*. The regional parties have behaved in a far worse manner, leading me to the pessimistic conclusion that liberalism is vulnerable and fragile in India.

As a middle-of-the-road liberal, I find I have no one to vote for. And yet I must. My fear is that one of the candidates will win.

Is there hope for a liberal party?

I mourn the death of the Swatantra Party. It was a wondrous, fleeting moment in our history that lasted only 15 years, from 1959 to 1974. It was the only true classical liberal party India ever had. Alas, it was ahead of its time. It was unique in not depending on 'identity' as its raison d'etre—a rare party of principle, unlike most Indian political parties, beginning with the Congress and the BJP, who are in a race to the bottom, competing to dole out freebies in order to get elected. It passionately fought the post-Independence command economy of the ruling Congress Party, and when it came to identity issues, such as language, it gave freedom to its members to vote as they wished without a party whip. At the time, it was dismissed by India's powerful left-leaning establishment as a 'CIA led, feudal clique of reactionaries'.

Swatantra was bound to fail, as Jaithirth Rao argues in a persuasive essay, 'The Problem with Liberal Parties' (in

Liberalism in India, ed. Parth Shah). In an exhaustive analysis of political parties in India and abroad, he concludes that in order to have a meaningful presence, parties inevitably fall back on identity—either region, language, caste or religion. Coalitions apparently are no different. Even the powerful Liberal Whigs in the UK, a major factor in British politics for two centuries, depended on their Low Church Protestant backgrounds, just as Tories depended on the Anglican High Church. The same has been the fate of liberal parties almost everywhere. There are exceptional periods when a party is so popular that it becomes a big tent, such as Nehru's Congress Party or F.D. Roosevelt's Democratic Party. But these are exceptions.

The unhappy conclusion I have reached is that it is almost impossible for a liberal party to get elected in India. Hence, the only option for a classical liberal is to join a mainstream political party and hope to change its agenda from within. This too is important. Although the debate on democratic freedom is rampant in democracies around the world, a discussion on economic freedom is conspicuously absent. At a minimum, it will help the public to understand the difference between a classical and a left liberal.

The liberal is unelectable

Having no one to vote for, I used to often get pessimistic about politics. Behind it lay a nagging guilt. I asked myself—had I taken the easy road in life, offering armchair commentary on politics and policies? Shouldn't I jump into active politics and do some of the heavy lifting? At the university, I had learned from reading Aristotle that civic action was the high road to virtue. Ancient Greeks called a person *idiotis* (the origin of the English word 'idiot') who did not engage in politics. By not joining politics, I may have been following the path of sheep, which meant that I deserved to be ruled by wolves.

It was my conscience that made me decide one day at the beginning of the millennium to take the plunge. The problem was, which party to join? Amartya Sen had suggested reviving the old Swatantra Party, but it didn't stand a chance. India already had too many parties. Only the two leading ones had any hope of getting elected nationally. They may be flawed, I argued, but I might be able to push them in the right direction. So, I decided to give it a try. My friend Suman Dubey set up a meeting with Sonia Gandhi of the Congress and my sister-in-law did the same with L.K. Advani of the BJP. In both cases, it turned out to be a fiasco.

I arrived at 10 Janpath filled with hope and enthusiasm. Mr George, Mrs Gandhi's secretary, warned me that meetings with the grand lady lasted strictly 20 minutes, and I should rise as soon as she got up. Mrs Gandhi opened the conversation with a smile and a question. Pointing to a story in that morning's paper on the coffee table, she asked what conceivable difference opening the insurance sector to foreign investors would make to a poor farmer. Wasn't the country wasting time over such frivolous things when we ought to be worrying about the farmers going hungry at night? I answered her politely, explaining how crop insurance would help farmers—how the competition from overseas insurance companies would make Indian companies more efficient. I was going on and on, till I realised that I was speaking to the air. She had lost interest long ago. It felt very odd talking to myself. I was too reform-minded for her taste.

Mr Advani was aware of my writings. He asked how I defined myself. I told him that I had been a socialist until I began working under the command economy of the license raj. It was so oppressive that I became a laissez-faire libertarian and joined the Swatantra Party.

'Ah, a market-wallah!' he exclaimed.

Yes, but I turned back a bit when I realised the

importance of governance. I was now a classical liberal, and was on the board of the Centre for Civil Society, a liberal think tank devoted to education reform.

'Is socialism such a bad thing?' he asked.

'Yes, if it means state ownership of business and extortionate tax rates.'

He preferred to think of socialism as a compassionate society. Both of us agreed that if socialism meant the state would ensure high-quality education and healthcare, no one could object. He asked about my views on Hindutva. I told him I was comfortable being a Hindu but I was uncomfortable with Muslim bashing. He smiled sadly, congratulating me on my frankness and clarity. It was clear—he too had little use of me.

Both Sonia Gandhi and L.K. Advani had quickly calculated that I had no chance at the polls. I too was relieved, I must confess. I am generally uncomfortable with politicians. They are thinking of the next election whereas I am thinking of the next generation. To both Mrs Gandhi and Mr Advani, I belonged to the tribe of the English-educated professional who wanted a taste of power. The tribe had been edged out of mass politics by the 1970s. Far worthier persons than I had failed at the polls: Manmohan Singh, Arun Jaitley, Nandan Nilekani and others had to be accommodated in the Rajya Sabha. (Shashi Tharoor is, perhaps, the exception that proves the rule.)

Liberals tend to focus on principles, politicians on winnability. They have little use for idealistic peddlers of ideas. When pitted against a populist candidate, who promises free electricity or free rations, a liberal reformer stands no chance. Nor have liberals been able to craft their message in political terms like Mahatma Gandhi. The fact is that the 'invisible hand' of Adam Smith is, in fact, invisible to the voter. It is hard to grasp how the self-interest of millions of business persons in the marketplace can lead to success of the whole society.

The pro-market liberals in India who went on to join the BJP in order to influence it from within, face this predicament daily. They are comfortable as long as the discussion is about foreign direct investment, tariff policy, tax rates, etc. When the agenda moves to Hindu Rashtra, cow protection and beef, they begin to squirm. The same applies to liberals in the Congress Party. They are happy discussing market-friendly reforms but are embarrassed when the party waives farmers' debts just ahead of the election or plays vote bank politics.

The sad conclusion: a liberal is unelectable.

Good and bad nationalism

For good or for bad, there is a nationalist government in power, and this raises another dilemma. A liberal is against tribalism, and nationalism is a form of tribalism. Hence, a liberal is suspicious of the kind of nationalism that arose in 19th-century Europe when modern states were formed on the basis of identity—of a single religion, or language, or ethnicity—and went on to become instruments of power and violence in the 20th century. This nationalism proclaimed one's country was superior, sought an enemy and excluded minorities. It drove European nations to colonise the world; it made Germany and Japan militaristic; it led the Nazis to murder six million Jews in the Holocaust. These were the tragedies of this narrow-minded nationalism.

There is a good nationalism, however. It can help a country to modernise, develop with a sense of urgency, as Japan did after the Meiji Restoration in 1867-68. It can bring diverse and plural peoples to unite to throw out an imperial foreign power, as was the case in India during its freedom struggle in the first half of the 20th century. Meiji Japan focused on giving excellent education to all Japanese children, instilling a sense of national unity that helped mould the modern Japanese personality. India was born in 1947 out of good nationalism without shedding an ounce of blood, and it happened in the shadows of Hitler, Stalin and Mao. That nationalism was Indian, not Hindu or Muslim. It was the creation of Mahatma Gandhi and his associates. He was able to capture the hearts and minds of ordinary people because he spoke to them through traditional words and symbols. He appealed to their imagination with an inclusive, civilisational concept of *sadharana dharma,* a universal ideal applicable to all human beings—leading to duties such as *ahimsa,* 'not hurting another', or *satya,* 'telling the truth'. Unlike the dharma of caste, this dharma of conscience resonated with all Indians. As a result, an incipient sense of unity began to emerge in the popular consciousness, uniting the multitudinous communities of the subcontinent into one national community

Unfortunately, Mahatma Gandhi died soon after Independence. None of the leaders after him was up to the task of selling the excellent idea of a modern secular republic based on the rule of law. Well-meaning Jawaharlal Nehru was too much of a Western oriented gentleman; he tried but failed to connect with the people as Gandhi had been able to. This is why the ordinary person still believes that the Constitution fell from heaven one day, and does not understand or own it. Tocqueville has taught us that underlying a liberal democracy is a moral consensus which is expressed daily in 'habits of the heart', which is why the great Sanskrit scholar called our Constitution a 'dharma text'. The political class as a whole has failed not only to create new 'habits of the heart' but also a sense of modern national community. This has led to a Hindu nationalism instead of an Indian nationalism. In Milestone 26 in Chapter 5, I tried to answer the question why Hindus, who are 80 per cent of India's population, felt insecure in their own country.

If bad nationalism is about power, a good nationalism is cherishing one's country's natural beauty, the memories of childhood, of a particular time, place and a way of life. Bad nationalism is about power, prestige and wanting to dominate others. Bad nationalists are haunted by the belief that the past can be altered. They feel the need to holler, and shout slogans to proclaim their country's greatness, which often reflects insecurity, low self-esteem and even a feeling of inferiority. Good nationalists are quietly confident, comfortable in their skin, aware of their nation's strengths and weaknesses. They even wonder why their love has to stop at the border, because they are humans first and citizens of nations afterwards.

Today, the world is witnessing the ill-fated rise of bad

nationalisms. They are all driven by a utopian vision of a past when 'we were great' before we were beset by irritating immigrants, foreign invaders and minorities. The result is an unhappy polarisation in society, as in India, caused by the notion of a pure Hindu past that began to decline when Muslims came and began to rule. It is typical nationalist history, driven by power and distrust of and hatred for the Other. The danger of bad nationalism is that it runs the risk of turning militaristic.

There is another form of negative nationalism that leads nations to conspiracy theories and paranoia. When I was working for a multinational company, I was sometimes its target. Both Indian and Latin American social scientists used to complain incessantly that their poverty and backwardness were the result of the misdeeds of world capitalism. Multinational companies like mine were the villain in their eyes. Raul Prebisch, the Argentine economist, had created a 'dependency theory', which argued that poor nations would always remain dependent on rich Western nations because of unequal terms of trade. It led to export pessimism and isolationist policies in many countries, including India. As a result, many Third World countries failed to participate in global export booms that began in the 1950s and '60s. The Asian miracle in the

1980s proved the dependency theory wrong as Asian tigers rose on the basis of the export of manufactured goods. Another danger of bad nationalism is that it finds someone else to blame for one's troubles.

Today, bad nationalism makes us suspicious of trade treaties. It is still not too late for India to benefit from the positive lessons of East Asia's international trade liberalisation. Although the world is moving against globalisation, India should reposition its *atmanirbhar,* or self-reliant, philosophy to mean not just 'make in India' but 'make in India for the world'. India needs to shed export pessimism, bring down tariffs, join the Regional Comprehensive Economic Partnership (RCEP), participate in global supply chains, and reorient its Production Linked Incentive Scheme (PLI) contracts to incentivise exports. Only thus will it bring about 'the great transformation' to become a middle-class country. Exclusivism and isolationism are bad, self-defeating ideas for nations and societies.

In my personal life I go further. I feel we all have multiple identities and we ought to resist privileging our national identity. For example, I am an Indian male, but I am also a Punjabi, a father of two, a writer, a vegetarian, a lover of Kishori Amonkar's music, a cheerleader of our liberal reforms, a fan of the Indian cricket team, and so on. I have different identities, and I choose a particular one depending on the context. While I am proud of my Indian identity, I don't feel that I have let the side down if I enjoy Thai green curry or Italian pasta, Bach's German baroque or Kurosawa's Japanese films. Our identities also change with time; some people even change their religion; others migrate and change their nationality. The point is that identity is a matter of reasoned choice. Unfortunately, a Hindu nationalist wants to force-fit me into an overarching, rigid religious, nationalistic identity that takes away this choice and impoverishes my plural human spirit.

I think of human beings as diamonds with many faces. Hate begins when we categorise people, choosing one face and ignoring the others. When we reduce people to one dimension, we encourage a fragmented view of humanity. Instead, we should celebrate our plural identities.

Why is the admirable idea of secularism failing us?

I was five years old at the Partition of India and I witnessed the senseless murder of a Muslim policeman; I also heard stories from my parents of how people cheerfully killed their neighbours in the name of religion. Ever since, I have firmly believed that religion should never enter the public space. Later in life I converted to liberalism, which defined secularism as the separation of religion and state. However, Indian secularists took exception to this Western idea of secularism, claiming that India was too steeped in religion, and hence its secularism had to be different. They celebrated the Indian secular ideal of of *sarva dharma samabhava*, or equal respect for all religions, unlike the liberal ideal of the separation of church and state. The Indian ideal sounds lofty and attractive but it may be the cause of some of the mess we are in today.

In actual practice, the Indian ideal has been translated to justify separate personal laws in matters pertaining to marriage, divorce, succession or inheritance for different religious communities. The egregious differences relate to how women are treated, and every so often, people have demanded a common civil code in the interest of gender justice. The Indian approach to secularism is also used by governments to justify the state subsidising Haj pilgrimages for Muslims, for example, leading to a clamour among Hindus for a similar subsidy to visit their pilgrimage sites. It involves the state in administering Muslim waqf boards, Hindu religious endowments and Sikh shrines, and results in some people feeling that the state is favouring one religion over another.

The most famous of these controversies relates to a dispute between Hindus and Muslims over a mosque, the Babri Masjid in Ayodhya, which was demolished amidst nationwide riots in 1992. The matter went up to the Supreme Court, which awarded in 2019 the site of the demolished mosque to Hindus for building a Ram temple as demanded by Hindu nationalists, but it also made a provision for building a mosque nearby on an alternative site in Ayodhya. Many hoped that the court judgement would draw a line to prevent the recurrence of disputes over religious sites in the future. That hope, however, was soon crushed. A district court in Varanasi ordered a survey of another mosque, the Mughal-era Gyanvapi Masjid, to confirm if there were Hindu religious artifacts under the site. The Archaelogical Survey of India followed up the judge's order and conducted a survey of the Gyanvapi complex in 2023 to determine if the mosque was constructed over the pre-existing structure of a Hindu temple. Its report concluded that a large Hindu temple had indeed existed at the spot before the construction of the mosque. The Varanasi court also allowed Hindus to worship inside a sealed basement of the Gyanvapi Masjid.

This has opened a Pandora's box with similar claims being made for other mosques across India. A petition has been filed in the Supreme Court seeking surveys of all prominent mosques that are over 100 years old, and has raised the prospect of unending religious strife. The liberal in me concludes that the Indian ideal of *sarva dharma samabhava*, while morally attractive, is too fragile and slippery. I'd be more comfortable with a strict wall of separation between religion and state. We need to privatise religion. I wonder why Hindu nationalists feel insecure in a country where 80 per cent of the people are Hindu. It is bizarre to want to take revenge on history, claiming it is payback time for Muslims for lording over the Hindus for 500 years. It doesn't make sense. I keep asking myself where the admirable idea of liberal secularism has failed us. A hypothesis that keeps knocking around in my head is that it might have something do with excessive individualism, a basic flaw of liberalism. Hindu nationalism may well be a cry for community, a deep desire for solidarity in an India moving rapidly from tradition to modernity.

The liberal English-speaking elite, which has ruled the nation for all but a few years since Independence, did not bother to fashion a new modernity truer to the spirit of a new nation. They adopted a thoughtless form of secularism without having an honest conversation with tradition. This may have contributed to the regrettable rise of Hindu nationalism. Ironically, while dreaming of a grand civilisational state, Hindu nationalists are trying to create a narrow-minded, identity-based European nation-state. Even more ironically, while these Hindu nationalists reject Partition and the making of an Islamic Pakistan, their demand for a 'Hindu Rashtra', a Hindu Nation, ends up justifying both.

It is not only the liberal in me that revolts against exploiting religion in the public space. It is also common sense. In the present age of radical, jihadi Islam, why would anyone want to make India's 200 million moderate Muslims feel insecure? The threat to India is not from without but from within. It would only take a few thousand insecure Muslim youth to join up with global Islamic terror to produce chaos, and quickly undo the vast gains made by our nation. This is not to excuse Jihadism, which is a toxic belief that until every person on Earth becomes a believer in Allah, the jihadi must continue the holy war. On simple, pragmatic grounds, it doesn't make sense to alienate the mostly restrained Muslims of India. Every Indian, every human being, deserves dignity and freedom from fear, intimidation and humiliation.

Class vs caste

The Dalit is a human being, but upper-caste prejudice treats him or her as less than human. Our Constitution tried to ensure that Dalits and the oppressed castes would be treated with equal dignity and equal rights. No one would govern another human being without his or her consent. It went further to allow for reverse discrimination for a temporary period in the form of reservations in state jobs and higher education. Its liberal hope was that in time, with broad prosperity, prejudice would fade away.

Hence, the liberal in me is at odds with the continuing dominance of caste in India's political life. It is ironic to see caste parties aggressively fighting on identity issues when India's democracy has delivered huge gains to the oppressed castes. Periodic elections created vote banks, which brought Dalit and and other backward castes political power, and they went on to rule many states for decades. This brought a social revolution, especially in the backward northern states. The liberal would have expected their concerns to turn eventually from caste to class; they would want to better themselves economically as well. I hoped that what democracy had done for the lower castes in the 20th century, capitalism would do in the 21st century. Once they realised that better jobs were in the private sector, not in the government, they would want to turn their demands from reservations to better education and healthcare.

A classical liberal is wary of group rights which privilege one community, compromising the principle of equality before the law. I was thus opposed initially to affirmative action based on reservations or quotas because it was a form of reverse discrimination. I used to believe that caste discrimination would go away in time as the oppressed castes moved up from poverty to the middle class. What really matters, after all, is (1) economic growth, which creates employment opportunities, raising people economically, and leads also to urbanisation and mobility, liberating them from discrimination in their 'casteist' village; and (2) access to good schools and primary health centres, which brings equality of opportunity at the start, giving everyone an equal chance to succeed in life. Hence, I was against reservations and quotas.

Soon, however, I realised that I was wrong. Caste discrimination has existed for thousands of years and is too entrenched in people's minds. It will not go away merely through economic development. People are not motivated only by material well-being, nor by political power; they also want status. Status trumps class in this case. Even though Dalits and other backward castes may have political power, they are still being discriminated against even in the cities. Discrimination is in the mind of the subject and the object. Oppressed persons internalise their low status, which shapes their feelings of self-worth. They buy into the myth of their inferiority, and behave as they are expected to, according to the stereotypes of incompetence.

Hence, I was wrong in my initial liberal view that once 'low-caste' persons rose out of poverty into the middle class, they would be free from discrimination. Thus, I became resigned to Ambedkar's idea of affirmative action as a temporary palliative to help the most underprivileged Dalits and tribals. What I did not expect was that once the Pandora's box of reservations opened, it would be impossible to close it in India's democracy. Even though half the positions in government jobs and seats in universities are reserved today, the clamour continues. Even dominant groups in the country are fighting in the race to the bottom, wanting to be declared backward. If the Congress Party had had its way in the previous coalition government, reservations would have been extended to the private sector. When will this nightmare come to an end?

The liberal fallacy

It is difficult to understand why government schools in India keep failing. There is universal consensus that education is not only good in itself, it also creates opportunities for all and helps a nation to become competitive. Even before 1991, when we had a socialist government in power, K-12 education was mostly ignored. This was inexcusable. After all, education is one of the few things that socialists around the world generally did well.

When I make this observation, my friends remind me that I am guilty of the liberal fallacy—that is, I naively assume that liberalism works by simply setting reason free. That is, reasoning will prevail over interests. Hence, I tend to get surprised when the opposite happens in the real world. The road to power is through satisfying interests. Reasoning about right and wrong policies is necessary, but is of limited use if you want to make things happen. It is not enough to point out the wrong policies, as liberals tend to do. You have to go further and trace bad policies to interests—both economic and political. Politicians in a democracy respond to what brings them votes.

Democracy is a short-term game and education is a long-term one. Politicians in a democracy are playing a Twenty20 cricket match while education is a test match.

Results in education take a long time to come. When a politician promises rice for two rupees a kilo when it costs five, he wins the election, as N.T. Rama Rao did in the 1994 state elections in Andhra Pradesh, and became chief minister. He immediately implemented his promise and went on to bankrupt the treasury. Since the 1980s, politicians in Punjab have vigorously competed in giving subsidised or free electricity to farmers. In a poor country, a populist with a bag full of freebies will always defeat a liberal reformer. When populists do that, where is the money to come from for creating new schools or improving old ones?

This is a dilemma liberal reformers in India have faced. It is why India reforms by stealth. Ever since 1991, no reformer has bothered to go before the public and educate it about how the market works, how market-based reforms help everyone, not just business. I admire Margaret Thatcher in Britain for having done this. It is not an easy task, because 'the invisible hand' of the market is also invisible to the voter. Reforming is a frustrating process in a democracy. Deng in China was perhaps the greatest reformer in history. But he had it easier—China was not a democracy.

Are markets moral?

Even people who are convinced that the market delivers greater prosperity do not think capitalism is a moral system. Most believe that morality depends on religion. This is not true. The fact is that human self-interest can go a long way to ensure good behaviour. A seller who does not treat his customers with fairness and civility will lose market share. A company that markets defective products will lose customers. A firm that does not promote the most deserving employees will lose talent to its competitors. A buyer who does not respect the market price will not survive. Lying and cheating will ruin a firm's image, making it untouchable to creditors and suppliers. Hence, free markets offer powerful incentives for ethical conduct, backed by state institutions that enforce contracts and punish criminal behaviour. You don't need religion for morality.

If the market is based on an inbuilt morality, why are there so many crooks in the marketplace? The answer is that in every society there is a natural distribution of crooked people, and the market has its share of them, which is why we need effective regulators, policemen and judges. We should design our institutions to catch crooks and not harass innocent people as we do too often.

Some Indians believe that capitalism has been forced

on us by the imperial West. This too is a mistake. Friedrich Hayek, the Noble laureate, called the market a 'spontaneous order'—it is natural for human beings to exchange goods and services—and in the process, every society evolved money, laws, conventions and morals to guide behaviour in the marketplace. These are natural products of human endeavour and not created by God. Nature's morality in the marketplace begins with the idea of freedom—the freedom of the individual to choose to buy or sell any product, or get a job of one's choosing. Competing and cooperating come naturally in the market economy, which has been with us in India for thousands of years. The bania had a respected place in society and he was accorded 'high-caste' status from the beginning.

People are suspicious of capitalism because they mistake 'self-interest' of the market for selfishness. A selfish person transgresses on the rights of others, but self-interest is not a social attribute and can be practised even on a deserted island. This is why Adam Smith called our desire to buy cheap and sell dear as rational self-interest. In the *Theory of Moral Sentiments,* he explained that what is *rational* is not only from the viewpoint of the interested person involved but also from that of a disinterested observer.

Whether we like it or not, India is headed in the

direction of some sort of democratic capitalism. It is important that we have a better opinion about the market and market-based reforms. It will be a sign of maturity one day when voters begin to dismiss short-term freebies in favour of long-term investment in areas such as education and health. This is how India will conquer pervasive poverty and become a developed nation.

The dilemma of a liberal Hindu

My wife and I were at dinner party in Delhi in 2004 when I mentioned casually to a left-leaning, former civil servant that I was planning to read the epic *Mahabharata*.

'Good God, man!' he exclaimed, 'You haven't turned Hindutva, have you?'

His remark was not made in jest. I asked myself what sort of secularism we had created that made reading a Sanskrit literary text a political act. I had to fear the intolerance of my 'secular' friends as much as the bigotry of the Hindu Right. Surrounded by narrow and rigid positions at both ends, it was difficult to be a liberal Hindu.

A few months later, an English friend visited us. On a shopping trip to Khan Market, we met a friend of our son. She wanted someone to explain an old figurine, and asked my son's friend if he was Hindu. His telling reply was, 'I am a Hindu, but ...', and he went into a winding reply. I sensed an unhappy defensiveness—the 'but' betrayed that he was almost ashamed of being Hindu.

Two years later, I was writing a book based on the *Mahabharata* when I got a call from one of Delhi's best schools, asking me to speak to its students. 'Oh good,' I replied, 'I shall speak about dharma and the moral dilemmas in the *Mahabharata*.' The principal was aghast. 'Oh don't, please!' She explained that there were important secularists on her governing board, and she didn't want a controversy about teaching religion. I protested. 'Surely, the *Mahabharata* is a literary epic, and dharma is about right and wrong. Where does religion come in?'

As I think about these incidents, I feel something has clearly gone wrong. With the rise in religious fundamentalism, it seems difficult to talk about one's deepest beliefs. Liberal Hindus are reluctant to admit to being Hindu for fear they will be automatically linked to Hindutva nationalists, who have appropriated Hindu culture, turning it into a political agenda. I also blame our secularists who have closed their minds to faith and tradition. I fear that young, modern Indians may not have any use for their past.

If Italian children can proudly read Dante's *Divine*

Comedy in school, and the English can read Milton's *Paradise Lost*—both with lots of mentions of God—why can't Indian children read the *Mahabharata?* I despair over the unhappy fact that young Indians are growing up ignorant of their rich past. Like Edmund Burke, I think of society not merely as a collection of loosely related individuals, but a living organism. A feeling of reverence for the past should not be a political doctrine but a habit of the mind, a way of living.

The defensiveness of Hindus about India's spiritual and humanistic heritage will diminish if young people have access to their great texts in a secular setting. These texts are not ideological weapons but rich sources of deliberation and understanding. Their study will nourish a questioning and tolerant spirit that will prevent them from being exploited by the ideological right wing. It will build in them a secular temper that values the continuity of history and tradition.

The dilemma of desire

A liberal prizes the idea of human agency. Each human being is an end in itself and hence should have the dignity and autonomy consistent with that ideal. This is why John Stuart Mill's 'The Subjection of Women' created such excitement among liberals in the 19th century. Mill clearly saw a link between liberty and equality. If some people are subjected to the will of others, the idea of human agency is violated. Caste violates this principle; so does the subjection of women. At the root of this subjection is man's fear of woman's desire. Sexual liberation in the 20th century has been a great victory precisely for women's desire.

In recent times in India, too, young middle-class Indians are becoming sexually liberated. The courts have also been supportive—decriminalising homosexuality, adultery and other acts in favour of gender equity. However, prudish conservatives are unhappy, reminding the young ceaselessly that such liberated attitudes are contrary to our ancient tradition. They are wrong! There was always a positive, confident strand in India's thinking about desire, as I have pointed out in chapter three.

At the end of that chapter, I write about an optimistic attitude to desire in ancient India. It originated as a life-force in the *Rig Veda*, and was elevated to a goal of life. Gradually, 'kama' became a romantic orientation to the world, spreading through the psychological life of human beings. It reached a peak in courtly life in the Gupta period (320 CE–550 CE), bringing about an early sexual liberation, which has left behind a rich inheritance of erotic and romantic culture in Sanskrit love poetry, Vatsyayana's *Kamasutra,* and in the visual arts.

True, there was also a pessimistic strand in the renouncer's attitude to desire. But the liberal Hindu should confidently stand up to the pessimistic conservative, and offer a legitimate defence based on the optimistic side of tradition.

The dilemma of a liberal Muslim

Moderate, well-educated Muslim liberal friends of mine face an even greater dilemma in India. They are caught between fanatics from both sides. Earlier, they had to confront extremists from their own orthodox community. Now they are also expected to prove to the Hindu nationalists that they are true Indians. Their secular space has diminished even more than a liberal Hindu's.

Some of them quickly grow defensive, such as a Muslim friend who visits me occasionally. He reminds me that the Quran does not speak of any 'Islamic state'; nor does it want me to stone adulterers, or punish those who drink alcohol or women who don't wear the hijab. But they dare not utter these things to a mullah or an orthodox Muslim. My friend feels let down by the lack of moderate Muslim leaders who can educate their community.

'I was born in India, and I have always believed that I was Indian,' he says. 'But why do I have to prove it to someone from the Bajrang Dal? Or to the immigration officer at the airport?' He goes on to talk about the toxic WhatsApp campaign that viciously attacks a Muslim daily. It is painful for him to read the lies they spread about history. I feel sympathy for him when he tells me about the difficulty his son is facing in renting an apartment in Gurgaon, just because he has a Muslim name.

'I don't want India to become a Hindu Pakistan!' he sighs.

He has a dim view of Pakistan and similar theocracies for a reason. I cannot agree with the Congress Party's line equating Hindu and Muslim fundamentalism, calling them two sides of the same coin. They are not—at least not yet. If my friend speaks out against Muslim extremists in his community, he risks his life. When I speak out against Hindu extremists of the saffron brigade, I am not in similar danger. I have done so on TV and nothing has happened to me. The most strident criticism against the demolition of the Babri Masjid came from Hindu commentators. My Muslim friend had no problem in reading Rushdie's *Satanic Verses*—in fact, he liked it—and he didn't think it ought to have been banned. But he would endanger his life if he admitted this in public. The truth is that a Muslim must also be able to speak up, just as a Hindu liberal does, in order to save India's secularism.

Do democracy, capitalism and liberalism go together?

I used to believe that democracy would inevitably bring prosperity to India. This has proved to be false. There is no such link. Dictatorships like China's can create economic miracles. During the first four decades of its history, India had a socialist command economy that performed very poorly. Since market liberalisation, both China and India have risen to become the world's fastest growing economies. Hundreds of millions have been lifted out of poverty and the middle class has grown immensely. While people have not benefitted equally, the average person is better off. Both nations have benefitted immensely from globalising capitalism—China has become the world's factory and India its back office. What matters for economic development is not political but economic liberty.

Another lesson I have learned is that political liberty is a good in itself and does not need anything (like prosperity) to justify it. Nor is there a necessary connection between democracy and liberalism. Democracies can be illiberal. Liberalism is about making the state accountable—shielding citizens, their beliefs and property, from the intrusive powers of the state. Democracies often throw up populist, autocratic leaders, who are willing to bend the rules. The duty of liberals is to remind them about the rule of law, the protections of civil liberties, and the right to dissent. A typical problem in democracy is the 'tyranny of the majority', which is why liberals insist upon checks and balances in state power, and protections for minorities.

Ironically, it is the rich West, especially the United States—the most vocal advocate of free market global capitalism—which is turning against the free market. In recent elections, Democrats in the US have made a major issue of 'outsourcing' of jobs to China and India. Similarly, Republicans have become protectionist, sloganeering about 'Make in America', bringing tariffs on goods and raising subsidies on agriculture. In contrast, Communist China has carried out massive unilateral trade liberalisation over the last 20 years. It is understandable that short-term losers from globalisation are employing politics to win votes. However, a better solution would have been to re-orient their own education systems to produce higher skilled people while providing targeted benefits to the deserving unemployed losers of globalisation.

Conclusion: What's next?

There is an unhappy discrepancy between the optimistic beginning of this book when liberalism was an irresistible force sweeping the world, and the unexpectedly bleak prospects for liberalism today. There are plenty of reasons to feel discouraged. Speaking as an Indian liberal, it has been sobering to realise that the liberal in India is neither electable, nor is there hope for a true liberal party. Worse, I have no one to vote for. I am thus on a lonely road. My nightmare is the possibility that illiberal democracy may be here to stay both in India and the world.

I have lost my friends on the left and the right; you have to be either pro- or anti-Modi, on the side of good or evil. Well, I refuse to see the world in black and white. The left is critical of my naive faith in the market and in globalisation. The right faults me for my allergy to nationalism and identity politics. The left has abandoned individual autonomy and free speech in favour of claims of group rights. On the right, the promoters of neoliberal economics have turned the ideal of individual autonomy and the free market into a religion. Both find me an incorrigible centrist, a dithering fence-sitter who can't make up his mind. In my defence, I maintain that both sides have closed their minds and I am unable to converse meaningfully with either. My liberal temper, however, refuses to give up on either side—I believe both have their uses. The left reminds me of the existence of the poor and the inevitability of inequality and oligopoly in the free market system. The right provides a reminder of the importance of community and solidarity. Unfortunately, both sides have an unhappy tendency to hand over power much too readily to the state.

I feel discouraged by politics in general as I weigh the liberal conundrum of the famous American author John Steinbeck: 'The things we admire in men, kindness and generosity, openness, honesty, understanding and feeling, are the concomitants of failure in our system. And those traits we detest, sharpness, greed, acquisitiveness, meanness, egotism and self-interest, are the traits of success. And while men admire the quality of the first, they love the produce of the second.'

Despite its gloomy prospects, I am unable to abandon my faith in liberalism. The answer is not to give up on liberalism but to remember that to be moderate is a virtue in politics. Yes, 'moderate' is hardly the kind of thing that gets people pouring into the streets. But liberalism's fundamental values of open-mindedness, tolerance, generosity and mutual respect are far too attractive to be abandoned by ordinary, decent human beings. The desire for maximum equal liberty and the rule of law is universal. Liberalism offers an appealing, ethically responsible human order, which is based on consent. Its open nature allows it to reform its own shortcomings. Because of so many virtues, I do not believe it can stay down for long. It has been in greater trouble before, having faced far more powerful enemies—fascism and communism—and it has prevailed in the end. Moreover, it has an excellent track record, having lifted a significant chunk of humanity in the past two centuries from oppression and hunger. Speaking as an Indian, it also resonates with our liberal civilisational temper. All these reasons convince me that it will prevail over the current illiberal populist, autocratic mood.

Thus, I cannot help but conclude this book on an optimistic note. Liberalism is ultimately an act of the imagination, says Lionel Trilling. Even in great adversity, human beings have the power to imagine a better future. It is important not to turn against politics or become passive. The present crisis is a call to action. Civic action is the high road to virtue and it is a duty to remain an active citizen. As I have said before, history tends to be cyclical, and eventually the rational side of human nature ought to, and will, re-assert itself.

SELECT BIBLIOGRAPHY

Bayly, C.A. *Recovering Liberties: Indian Thought in the Age of Imperialism and Empire* (2012)

Bell, Daniel *The Cultural Contradictions of Capitalism* (1976)

Bell, Daniel *The End of Ideology* (1960)

Bellah, Robert *Habits of the Heart: Individualism and Commitment in American Life* (1985)

Bellamy, Richard *Rethinking Liberalism* (2000)

Berlin, Isaiah, 'Two Concepts of Liberty', in Isaiah Berlin, *Four Essays on Liberty* (1969)

Berlin, Isaiah *Liberty*, Henry Hardy, (ed.) (2016)

Dalton, Dennis, *Indian Ideas of Freedom* (2023)

Dworkin, Ronald *Sovereign Virtue* (2000)

Dworkin, Ronald *Takings Rights Seriously* (1978)

Fawcett Edmund *Liberalism: The Life of an Idea* (2014)

Friedman, Milton *Capitalism and Freedom* (1962); Anniversary edition (2002)

Fukuyama, Francis *Liberalism and its Discontents* (2022)

Fukuyama, Francis, 'The End of History?', *National Interest* (1989)

Galston, William A. *Liberal Purposes: Goods, Virtues, and Diversity in the Liberal State* (1991)

Gandhi, M. K. *Hind Swaraj & Other Writings*, Ed. Anthony J. Parel (1997)

Ganguly, Swagato, 'Community Publics and the Republic: India's Ambivalent Secularism', *India in Transition, 10 October 2022*

Guha, Ramachandra, 'The Absent Liberal: An Essay on Politics and Intellectual life' *Economic and Political Weekly*, January 2001

Guha, Ramachandra *Democrats & Dissenters* (2016)

Ghose, Sagarika *Why I am a Liberal: A Manifesto for Indians Who Believe in Individual Freedom* (2018)

Hartz, Louis *The Liberal Tradition in America* (1955)

Hayek, F.A. *The Road to Serfdom*; New edition (2008)

Huntington, Samuel, 'The Clash of Civilizations?', *Foreign Affairs* (Summer 1993)

Khilnani, Sunil *The Idea of India* (1997)

Laski, Harold The *Rise of European Liberalism* (1936)

Locke, John *Two Treatises on Government* (1690)

Mehta, Pratap Bhanu *The Burden of Democracy* (2003)

Meinardus, Ronald *How Liberal is India: The Quest for Freedom in the Biggest Democracy on Earth* (2019)

Manent, Pierre *An Intellectual History of Liberalism* (1995)

Marx, Karl and Engels, Friedrich *The Communist Manifesto* (1848)

Marx, Karl *Grundrisse: Foundations of the Critique of Political Economy* (1939)

Mehta, Uday Singh *Liberalism and Empire: A Study in Nineteenth-Century British Liberal Thought* (1999)

Mill, John Stuart *On Liberty* (1859)

Mill, John Stuart *Three Essays on Religion* (1874)

Mill, John Stuart *The Subjection of Women* (1869)

Mukherjee, Rudhrangshu *Twilight Falls on Liberalism* (2019)

Nozick, Robert *Anarchy, State and Utopia* (1974)

Paine, Thomas *Common Sense, Rights of Man, and Other Essential Writings* (1776)

Rawls, John *A Theory of Justice* (1971)

Rawls, John *Political Liberalism* (1993)

Ryan, Alan *The Making of Modern Liberalism* (2012)

Said, Edward *Orientalism* (1978)

Sen, Amartya *Development and Freedom* (1999)

Sengupta, Hindol *The Liberals* (2012)

Shah, Parth ed. *Liberalism in India: Past, Present and Future* (2016)

Siedentop, Larry *Inventing the Individual: The Origins of Western Liberalism* (2014)

Smith, Adam *An Inquiry into the Nature and Causes of the Wealth of Nations* (1776)

Steinbeck, John *Cannery Row* (1945)

Schumpeter, J.A. *Capitalism, Socialism and Democracy* (1950)

Tagore, Rabindranath *The Religion of Man* (1931)

Tocqueville, Alexis de *Democracy in America* (1945)

Trilling, Lionel *The Liberal Imagination* (1950)

Walzer, Michael 'The Communitarian Critique of Liberalism', *Political Theory*, vol 18, No I, 1990

Wolff, Robert Paul *The Poverty of Liberalism* (1968)

Zakaria, Fareed *The Future of Freedom: Illiberal Democracy at Home and Abroad* (2003)

ACKNOWLEDGEMENTS

This book originated as the Third Annual Liberals Lecture by the same title that I delivered on 4 September 2023 at the India International Centre in Delhi. It was sponsored jointly by the Centre for Civil Society and the Friedrich Naumann Foundation. I am grateful to both for having given me the opportunity. Present at the lecture was a friend, Ravi Singh. I'd known him from his days at Penguin, and he had since gone on to found Speaking Tiger Books, a respected independent publishing house. He liked the lecture and wanted to publish it before the 2024 general election. Initially, I was reluctant as I generally take years over a book. But the subject was close to my heart, and so it didn't take much persuading. In a moment of reckless bravado, I agreed. This is how this modest, essay-size book was born.

ACKNOWLEDGEMENTS

My happiest task is to thank the generous souls who have helped along the way. To begin with, I owe a debt to the many thinkers whose ideas have shaped my thinking over the years. They are mentioned in the select bibliography. Then there are friends who took the trouble to read the manuscript or at least parts of it, and offer comments. Here they are in no particular order: Shruti Rajpal, Nimai Mehta, Swagato Ganguly, Janaki Kathpalia and Luis Miranda.

www.ingramcontent.com/pod-product-compliance
Lightning Source LLC
LaVergne TN
LVHW050406160726
843469LV00041B/978

* 9 7 8 9 3 5 4 4 7 6 7 9 2 *